The Sinners's Guide
by
The Venerable Louis of Granada

I highly recommend *The Sinner's Guide* but to read it
fruitfully don't run through it hastily. Ponder it and feel its
full weight. Muse upon each chapter and apply it to your
soul with thoughtfulness and prayer. Read it with reverence
and devotion, like a book containing the most useful
inspirations you can receive from on high, and thereby
reform all the powers of your soul.

St. Francis de Sales

The Sinner's Guide converted over a million souls during
my lifetime. St. Teresa of Avila

Abandonment to
Divine Providence
by
Fr Jean-Pierre de Caussade, SJ

The Sinner's Guide
and
Abandonment to Divine Providence
by
Brother Bob

Copyright 2011
WordWright.biz
ISBN 1-934335-48-2 (10-digit)
ISBN 978-1-934335-48-2 (13-digit)

A Christian Classic Imprint

Coming Soon!
**Other Books in the Christian
Classics Series for
21st Century Christians**

*An Introduction to the Devout Life
by St. Francis de Sales*

*An Imitation of Christ
by Thomas a Kempis*

*The cover art is from an unsigned painting that has
special significance for Brother Bob.
He found this unsigned painting hanging in the home
of a friend and has no idea of who painted it. But
Brother Bob wishes to thank God for the talent He
gave to this artist, and to the artist himself for having
painted this beautiful work.*

Dedicated to the authors of these books,
The Venerable Louis of Granada, O.P.
and
Father Jean-Pierre de Caussade, S.J.

Table of Contents

Publisher's Note

This volume contains two classic books of Christian literature: *The Sinner's Guide*, and *Abandonment to Divine Providence*. Both books, though written centuries ago, contain basic Christian thought still relevant for our time. A problem arises, however, when the modern reader wishes to read them because they contain awkward and difficult to read sentences filled with long forgotten cultural references.

To remedy that situation, the author of this book has updated the language to a crisp 21st century style appropriate for modern readers.

We hope that you'll learn from these Christian classics and take them to heart for your own life. When you finish reading them and understand the concepts, we encourage you to read their older English translations and original language versions. These provide rich teachings and nuances where you can explore their depths more fully.

The Publishers

Introduction

These two books provide an amazing opportunity for you to lead a fulfilling Christian life. The first one, *The Sinner's Guide* by Venerable Louis of Granada, OP. provides a foundation for *Abandonment to Divine Providence*. You'll learn what things God wants you to do and not to do and why. In short, you'll see how everything in your life fits together to lead you closer and closer to God.

Once you've grasped these concepts you'll be ready to continue your journey. *Abandonment to Divine Providence* by Fr. Jean-Pierre de Caussade, SJ will help you listen to God and recognize how He constantly reaches out to you. You'll learn how to hear Him and accept all that He sends, both the good and bad. You'll come to realize that He sends you every new circumstance to draw you closer to Him.

These books provide wonderful opportunities for meditations and thoughtful prayer. You'll likely enjoy reading a page or two every day and look upon them as dear friends who provide wonderful counsel in good times and bad.

Brother Bob

The Sinner's Guide
by
Venerable Louis of Granada, OP

Chapter 1

The First Motive which obliges us to practice Virtue and to serve God: His Being in itself, and the excellence of His Perfections

Practice virtue because nothing pleases God more. Virtue, the very essence of God, embraces His infinite majesty, goodness, mercy, justice, wisdom, omnipotence, excellence, beauty, fidelity, immutability, sweetness, truth, and His inexhaustible riches and perfections.

In addition, God holds all beings in His power. He disposes of them as He wills while simultaneously commanding the winds, changing the seasons, guiding the elements, distributing the waters, controlling the stars, and creating all things. In short, as King and Lord of the universe, He maintains and guides everything, and every creature, everywhere.

St. Augustine sheds some light on the greatness of God when he said that if the whole world were full of empty books, and all the seas turned to ink, and every creature began writing, the books would fill, the seas would drain, and the writers would drop from exhaustion before they expressed any of God's perfection.

God's perfection provides the chief reason to love, serve, and admire Him. However, you can never sufficiently do these things because as St. Augustine observed, God always remains profoundly hidden though present everywhere. St. Gregory concluded that words can't express God's perfection and we only eloquently praise Him when in mute wonder.

If you need further proof of the infinite power and greatness of God, contemplate the order and beauty of creation. Consider the admirable order, marvelous beauty, and incomprehensible grandeur of the universe. Stars millions of times larger than the earth fill the sky and millions of creatures all over the world live so perfectly that none possess anything superfluous or not suited to their survival.

Moreover, God created this vast and majestic universe by a single act of His will. According to St. Denis, an effect is directly proportional to its cause, so imagine the greatness of the cause of creation. Fill with admiration and astonishment when contemplating His greatness. His creation provides a hint of the grandeur and incomprehensibility of His power. Thus, obey, fear, and revere Him.

You have a great obligation to love your God of goodness and infinite majesty. I view with incredulity how so many, for base pleasure, hate their neighbors and continually offend God. Some go even further and sin without any of these motives, through pure malice or habit. What incomprehensible blindness, stupidity, and rashness!

Thus, this first motive obliges you to love and serve God. An obligation so great that compared to it, all other obligations pale into insignificance. As does your guilt for offenses against people compared to the guilt you've incurred by your many sins against God.

Chapter 2

The Second Motive which obliges us to practice Virtue and to serve God: Gratitude for our Creation

Your creation obligates you to serve God because you always remain in debt to Him. If you don't, you incur the guilt of theft and ingratitude. When a person builds a house, they expect to profit by it. Who owns the fruit of a vine if not the one who planted it? Who should children serve, if not their parents?

Curiously, you can only return to God what you've received from Him. Imagine what He thinks of those who make no return and use His gifts to offend Him. We see God's reaction to this type of behavior in Ezekiel 29:3 when God says to the King of Egypt, "See! I am coming at you, Pharaoh King of Egypt, great crouching monster amidst your Niles, Who says, 'The Niles are mine; it is I who made them!'" For Pharaoh to claim rivers as his own when God created them represents the arrogance of anyone claiming their own self-importance and refusing to recognize their obligation to serve their Maker.

Your creation provides the foundation for all your other benefits as part of a virtuous feedback cycle. When you show your gratitude to God via living a holy life, following His commandments and doing good works, you don't provide Him any advantage because He doesn't need these things. However, because of His unlimited love for you when you live such a life, you merit other graces from His infinite goodness, which in turn you show your gratitude for, receive more graces, and so on.

The Old Testament teaches that whenever God bestowed a favor upon His people He immediately commanded them to celebrate and remember it. When He brought the Israelites out of Egypt He commanded them to commemorate it by a solemn festival every year their happy deliverance from bondage. When He slew the firstborn of the Egyptians and spared the Israelites, He commanded that in return they consecrate their firstborn to Him. When He sent them manna from Heaven to sustain them in the wilderness, He ordered them to put a portion of it in a vessel and keep it in the tabernacle as a memorial to His extraordinary love.

Since God requires a continual remembrance of His favors, He requires gratitude for giving us our immortal souls. St. Augustine, speaking on this subject, said that we should think of God as often as we breathe because our being is continuous and immortal.

Perhaps you believe that all your benefits come by chance or nature rather than from God and you ask why you owe gratitude for the natural order of the world. This objection isn't worthy of a Christian, a pagan, or any reasonable person. The philosopher Lucius Seneca addressed this when he said, "You say that you receive all benefits from nature. Senselessness, you've merely changed the name of God because nature is God Himself. Therefore, it is no excuse to think that you're indebted to nature because without God there is no nature. If you received a loan from me, Lucius

Seneca, you wouldn't dare to say that you owed Lucius and not Seneca. Such a subterfuge would change my name, but wouldn't cancel your debt!"

Thus, gratitude for your creation obliges you to serve God, and your necessities drive you to Him to attain the perfection and happiness for which He created you. Remember, God didn't create you in a state of perfection but rather in a state of sin and you must cultivate your virtues throughout your lifetime. All living things instinctively go back to their first cause for their development and perfection. Plants unceasingly seek the sun and sink their roots deep into the earth where they first grew. Fish don't leave the water where they were born. Baby chicks seek the life-giving warmth and shelter beneath their mother's wings and baby lambs cling to their mother's side. All these living things and millions more, with blind instinct, seek what they lack at the source where they received all that they are.

Yes, God may let you go hungry so that driven by necessity you seek comfort in Him. For this reason, He didn't create you perfect because He loves you. He doesn't want you poor, but poverty helps make you humble and He doesn't want you hurting, but rather to have reason to seek Him.

He alone satisfies and never fails you. With Him, you can find contentment in poverty, richness in destitution, and happiness in solitude. Rich indeed is the poor man like St. Francis of Assisi, who though owning nothing, had God for his inheritance. The wealth and power of the rich, who don't serve God, fall prey to anxieties they can't calm, and suffer appetites they can't satisfy. Expensive clothes, big homes, and huge bank accounts can't calm a troubled mind. Therefore, God's gift of creation obliges you to serve Him to attain happiness and perfection.

Chapter 3

The Third Motive which obliges us to serve God: Gratitude for our Preservation and for the Government of His Providence

Preservation provides the third reason to serve God. God created and preserves you and you can't exist without Him, just like you couldn't create yourself. The benefit of preservation surpasses that of creation because creation happens as a single act, while preservation continues for eternity. So if your Creator demands great gratitude, imagine what you owe for the gift of preservation. You don't blink an eye, nor take a step without His power. How then can people deliberately continue to offend their benefactor?

It reminds me of the man on the top of a high tower suspending someone with a small cord over an abyss. Do you think the latter would dare yell nasty words to the one suspending him in midair? How then do so many people, whose existence hangs by threads held by God, dare to make Him angry?

St. Dennis points out that God has so much goodness, that even though people offend and rebel against Him, He continues to give them the power and strength that they use to resist Him.

A time will come when God will punish those who close their eyes to the sweet light of His mercy and they'll groan under the severity of His justice when the time for repentance passes. We live surrounded by the proof of His love, and yet many never think of Him. Millions feed like a herd of swine under an oak tree while their keeper showers down acorns. They greedily grunt and quarrel while never raising an eye to their master. Beware, lest God make this terrible accusation against you at the hour of your death! The more you've perverted His benefits, the more exacting the account you'll have to make.

Chapter 4

The Fourth Motive which Obliges us to Practice Virtue: Gratitude for the Inestimable Benefit of our Redemption

By a single act of His will, God created the whole universe without diminishing His treasures or power. He created an earthly paradise where we lived in harmony with Him. This should have bound us to Him with love and gratitude for the graces He bestowed on us. However, we boldly rebelled against Him and for this, God expelled us from paradise and condemned us to grovel in the dirt, suffer, and live and die without knowing Him.

Having brought misery upon ourselves, God felt more compassion for our pitiful condition than anger for our despicable rebellion. He resolved to reconcile us to Him through the mediation of His only Son. Through Christ, God pardoned our sins and restored us to His grace. In all of creation, no union compares with this union of grace, love and person. God created the universe in an instant, but to redeem it, He labored thirty-three years, shed the last drop of His Blood, and suffered incredible pain and anguish. Thus, He established our peace and remedied our miseries.

You owe the Lord infinite gratitude for doing this. You

owe even more gratitude for the way He performed this wonder. He endured such pain and suffering that the very thought of Him bathed in sweat and blood should overwhelm you. Confess your inability to understand this incomprehensible mystery and open your heart to His boundless love, and make a corresponding return. Though you can never hope to repay Him fully, return His tears with your tears and His life with your life.

Many show more ingratitude than savage beasts. St. Ambrose told a story about a dog that witnessed his master's murder. All night the faithful animal remained by the body, howling and crying. The next day, some people visited the scene and the dog spotted the murderer among them. The dog attacked the man with rage and this led to the discovery of his crime. If a dog can show such indignation against his master's murderer, how can you look with indifference on the murderers of your sovereign Lord?

Sadly, look at yourself as one of His murderers. Yes, your sins apprehended, bound, and nailed Him to the cross. His executioners couldn't have done this without the fatal aid of your sins. Accept responsibility for this and increase your love for Him. All that He did and suffered, He did to produce in your heart a horror and hatred of sin. Tremble at the thought of sin, and never dare to offend God and remain insensible to the terrible and appalling sight of God nailed to a cross. Always show supreme gratitude for the amazing gift of your redemption.

Chapter 5

The Fifth Motive which obliges us to practice Virtue: Gratitude for our Justification

Justification banishes sin from your soul, reconciles you to God, and restores His friendship. Justification delivers you from misfortune and restores you to God's grace by the most intimate love of a parent for a child.

Justification also saves you from the eternal pain of Hell. By our sin, we disobeyed God and drove Him away. God in return closed the gates of Heaven and condemned us to the eternal pains of Hell and the torment of guilt that gnaws at the conscience of sinners. Consider also the confusion and darkness of your existence, where you find little rest, joy, or peace but much anger, blasphemies, and sorrow. Thankfully, God saves those He justifies from these torments.

Sin deprives your soul of God's grace, and the more numerous your sins, the greater the destruction of your soul. Sin renders your soul miserable, cowardly in resisting temptation, and neglectful in the observance of God's commandments. Sin makes you a slave to the world, the flesh, and the devil. Sin can so dull and stupefy your spiritual senses that you no longer hear God's voice. You'll fail to see dreadful threatening calamities, not recognize the sweet odor of virtue, become incapable of tasting the sweetness of the Lord, and fail to feel the touch of His benign hand. Sin destroys the peace and joy of your conscience, takes away your soul's fervor, and makes you abominable in the eyes of God.

God, via the grace of justification, delivers you from all these miseries. In His infinite mercy, He wants to do more than forgive and restore you to His favor. He wants to restore you to your former strength and beauty. He heals your wounds, breaks your bonds, restores the supernatural beauty of your soul, re-establishes the peace and joy of your conscience, inspires you with ardor for good and a hatred of sin, and enriches you with an abundance of good works.

Justification also transforms your soul into a living member of Christ, thus providing a new source of graces and privileges. Jesus infuses into you the virtue of His life, and continually guides and directs you. Our Heavenly Father tenderly looks upon such souls as members of His Divine Son, united to Him by the participation of the Holy Spirit. Your works please God because Jesus lives and acts in them. Then you can confidently address God in prayer because you pray not so much for yourself but for His Divine Son because the honor of your life redounds to Him.

Justification provides the gift of eternal life. God has infinite mercy, and while He condemns impenitent sinners to eternal misery, He rewards the truly repentant with eternal happiness. God could have pardoned and restored us to His favor without allowing us to share in His glory. However, in the magnificence of His mercy, He adopts those He pardons, justifies those He adopts, and allows them to partake in the inheritance of His Son. The hope of this incomparable inheritance comforts the just in all their tribulations for they feel God's love even in the midst of difficult situations.

No one can be certain of justification, yet when you change your life, you see its possibility. Someone who previously committed innumerable sins and who now wouldn't dream of doing anything wrong provides such an example. For all these graces, unite your voice with the prophet, saying, "My mouth shall be filled with your praise, shall sing your glory every day." (Ps. 71:8)

Chapter 6

The Sixth Motive which obliges us to practice Virtue: Gratitude for the Incomprehensible Benefit of Election

To all these benefits, I add election, which belongs to those God has chosen from all eternity to partake in His glory. The Apostle Paul gave thanks for this when he said, "Blessed be the God and Father of our Lord Jesus Christ, who has blessed us in Christ with every spiritual blessing in the heavens, as He chose us in Him, before the foundation of the world, to be holy and without blemish before Him. In love He destined us for adoption to himself through Jesus Christ in accord with the favor of His will." (Eph. 1:3-5)

I call election the grace of graces, because God in His limitless goodness gives everything we need for salvation before we merit it. Therefore, all who recognize in themselves any sign of election must bless God for this great and eternal benefit. Though election often remains hidden, perseverance in doing good provides a sign of election. Those who live a number of years in the fear of God carefully avoiding sin, should pray, "He'll keep you firm to the end, irreproachable on the day of our Lord Jesus Christ." (1Cor. 1:8)

This great and wonderful gift deserves your highest

gratitude. God Himself tells His Apostles, "Nevertheless, don't rejoice because the spirits are subject to you, but rejoice because your names are written in heaven." (Lk. 10:20) What a blessing to have a privileged place in His Heart since the beginning of time, to have been chosen as His child before the birth of His Son, and to have been always present to His Divine Mind.

Weigh all the circumstances of this election and you'll see extraordinary favor in all of them and reasons to love and serve God. Consider first God's greatness. God, infinitely rich and infinitely happy, had no need of you or any other creature. Next, consider your unworthiness for such a gift, a miserable creature filled with infirmities and deserving eternal torment by virtue of your sins. Consider how this gift preceded all merit on your part, and sprang solely from the good pleasure and mercy of God. Remember, the more gratuitous the favor, the greater the obligation it imposes. Reflect on how God conferred this incredible benefit on you. He purchased it for you with the life and blood of His only Son.

Thus, you owe God tremendous gratitude and provided you do the necessary things for salvation, you can consider yourself a member of His happy group.

Chapter 7

The Seventh Motive for practicing Virtue:
The Thought of Death

Any of the motives presented so far provide sufficient reason, out of a sense of gratitude, to give yourself wholly to God. However, people generally approach life motivated by self-interest rather than from a sense of justice. Fortunately, practicing virtue in the interest of self provides advantages as well. The greatest reward for a life of virtue, eternal glory also provides us with an escape from the greatest punishment, damnation to Hell. Glory and punishment propel you in your voyage to eternity. For this reason, St. Francis and St. Dominic commanded their preachers to make vice and virtue, reward and punishment, the only subjects of their sermons to inspire people to lead virtuous lives.

Eternal glory and eternal misery correspond closely with death and judgment, which precede them. They provide powerful motivation to love virtue and hate vice, for Scripture says, "In all your works remember your last end, and you shall never sin." (Eccl. 7:40)

Your approaching death speaks powerfully to this topic. You'll face your particular judgment when your soul separates from your body and you receive your eternal judgment. Bear in mind that after death, you immediately render an account of your life. No one, whether rich or poor, escapes this moment. A day will come when you won't see the night, or a night when you won't see the morning.

No one knows the date of this event and Holy Scriptures say that it comes like a thief in the night. Often just before this event, grave illness with its weariness, sufferings, and pains weakens the body and allows entrance to the king of terrors who can rob you of all hope. The coldness of death seizes your body. Your skin grows deathly pale. Your tongue refuses to perform its duty. All your senses fall into confusion in anticipation of your departure. The parting from all you hold dear begins to rise before you. Wife, children, friends, relations, honors, and riches slip from your feeble grasp. Death with its vanguard of sickness breaks down the strength of your body, and just before the soul falls to the repeated assaults of the enemy, it takes flight from the ruins.

In the final days and hours, your terrified soul beholds the approach of the agony that will terminate its temporal existence. The horror and darkness of the grave dances in your mind, where you'll become the prey of worms. Keener still rages your suffering from the suspense and uncertainty of your approaching fate.

You'll imagine your presence with Jesus and see your sins rise up to accuse and condemn you. The evils you committed with so much indifference will fill you with terror. You'll curse a thousand times the days you sinned and the shameful pleasures that caused your ruin. You'll wonder to yourself, "How could I, for love of foolish things, face the torments that now await me?" The guilty pleasures will have long since passed away, but their terrible and irrevocable punishment will continue to stare you in the face. Side-by-side with this appalling eternity of misery, you'll see the unspeakable and everlasting eternal happiness you sacrificed.

Fear, the most powerful passion, magnifies trifles and makes remote evils appear close. Since slight apprehensions have this effect, imagine the power of the terror inspired by the great imminent danger of death. You, though still alive and surrounded by friends, imagine yourself already a prey to the torments of the devil. Your soul rips at the sight of the possessions you must leave, and you increase your misery by envying those you must leave. The sun rises in the morning, but wherever you look, darkness reigns. No ray of light or hope brightens your horizon. If you think of God's mercy, you believe you've no claim to it. If you think of God's justice, you tremble in fear. You feel your time has passed and God's time has come. If you look back on your life, a thousand accusing voices sound in your ears. If you turn to the present, you find yourself stretched upon a bed of death. If you look to the future, you see God waiting to condemn you. You desperately need a way to free yourself from so many miseries and terrors.

Everything fills you with terror and remorse. Your life has nearly ended and you believe no time for repentance remains. You don't see how your loved ones or friends can provide any help. What will you think at this supreme hour? Who will help you? To go forward will cause anguish, to go back impossible, and God won't permit you to continue. At the sight of your sins, and at the approach of God's justice, you already believe God has abandoned you. Though life remains with its opportunities for penance and reconciliation, fear drives hope from your heart, and in this miserable state, you breathe your last sigh in the darkness of despair.

Your eyes no sooner close in death than you appear before the judgment seat of God to render an account of every thought, every word, and every action of your life. To understand the severity and rigor of this judgment, don't ask those who live according to the spirit of this world, for they live in darkness and make sport of the most fatal errors. Rather, consult people enlightened by the true Sun of Justice, ask the saints and they'll teach you how hard it will be.

Saint Arsenius at his death experienced such great terror at the thought of God's judgment that his disciples, who knew the sanctity of his life, marveled in astonishment and said to him, "Father, why do you fear death?" To this he replied, "My children, this is no new fear for me. It is one that I've known and felt during my whole life." St. Agatho, at the hour of death, experienced similar terror and when asked why he, who had led such a perfect life, was afraid, answered, "The judgments of God are different from the judgments of men."

St. John Climacus gave a striking example of a holy monk named Stephen who lived in the desert and had a great desire to embrace a more solitary life. He had a reputation for sanctity. He also had the gift of tears and fasting and other privileges attached to the most eminent virtues. Having obtained his superior's permission, he built a cell at the foot of Mount Horeb, where Elias saw God. Though he led a very holy life, he desired harder labors and greater perfection so he withdrew to a place called Siden. Here he continued for some years in the practice of the most severe penance, cut off from all human contact or comfort seventy miles from any human habitation. As his life approached its end, he returned to his first cell at the foot of Mount Horeb where two disciples lived. Shortly after his arrival, he grew very sick with a fatal illness. The day before his death, he fell into a state resembling ecstasy. He gazed first at one side of his bed, then at the other and as if engaged in conversation with invisible beings demanding an account of his life. He cried out in a loud voice, "It is true, I confess it, but I have fasted many years in expiation of that sin," or, "It is false. That offense can't be laid to my charge," or again, "Yes, but I have labored for the good of my neighbor many years in atonement for that." To other accusations he said, "Alas! I can't deny it. I can only cast myself upon God's mercy."

St. John Climacus finished the story by saying, "What a thrilling spectacle! I can't describe the terror of witnessing this invisible judgment. Oh God! What will be my fate if this faithful servant, whose life of one long penance, couldn't answer some of the accusations brought against him?"

Dread your last hour and supreme tribunal. If just men tremble at this hour, how great is the terror of those who don't prepare for it, who spend their lives in the pursuit of vanities and in contempt of God's commandments?

Reflect then, on the moment you'll stand before the tribunal of God, with no defenders but your good works, with no companion but your conscience. At that moment, God will determine your fate for eternity, an eternity of happiness or an eternity of misery. Your tears won't soften Him and the time for repentance will have passed.

The unhappy soul can only exclaim with the prophet, "I was caught by the cords of death; the snares of Sheol had seized me; I felt agony and dread." (Ps. 116:3) You unhappy wretch. How swiftly this hour will come upon you. What does it matter that you had friends, or honors, or dignities or wealth? The wealth you hoarded will now go to others to squander, while your sins pursue you into the next world and condemn you to eternal torments. Why didn't you prepare for this hour? Why did you ignore all the warnings?

To preserve you from these regrets, I beg you to consider

the terrible remorse your sins will cause you at the hour of death. How ardently and vainly you'll wish that you had faithfully served God during your lifetime. Finally, how you'd willingly accept the most rigorous penance if God gave you one more chance. Acting on these considerations, begin now to live in a way that won't leave you with regrets. Take your one more chance now.

Chapter 8

The Eighth Motive for practicing Virtue: The Thought of the Last Judgment

The previous chapter presented the particular judgment that occurs immediately after death. Apostle Paul also spoke about a day of general judgment when he taught, "For we must all appear before the judgment seat of Christ, so that each one may receive recompense, according to what he did in the body, whether good or evil." (2Cor. 5:10) The Apostle Matthew said, "I tell you on the day of judgment, people will render an account for every careless word they speak. By your words you'll be acquitted, and by your words you'll be condemned." (Matt. 12:36) You must give an account of both your idle words that harm no one, as well as your impure words, immodest actions, sinful glances, blood-stained hands, and for all the time spent in sinful deeds.

Shame will overwhelm you when the final judgment exposes to the world your impurities, excesses, and sins hidden in the secret recesses of your heart. If you find it difficult to make known your sins in the secrecy of the confessional and prefer to groan under their weight, how will you bear to see them revealed to the universe?

Consider also the terror of sinners when this terrible sentence resounds in their ears: "...depart from me, you accursed, into everlasting fire which was prepared for the devil and his angels." (Matt. 25:41) Then their bodies will burn in a never-ending fire. The darkness will resound with despairing cries, blasphemies, perpetual weeping and gnashing of teeth. Sinners, in their rage, will tear their flesh and curse the inexorable justice that condemns them to these torments. They'll curse the day of their birth.

St. John Chrysostom frequently used this truth to encourage living lives of virtue. He taught to make your soul a temple of the Lord, and never lose sight of the solemn day when you'll appear before Christ to give an account of all your works. Save yourself from terrible misfortune before it is too late by making a humble and sincere confession.

Therefore, save your soul so it can share eternal happiness with your body. At the general judgment, it won't help to say, "Wealth dazzled me," or, "The world deceived me." The inexorable Judge will answer, "I warned you against these. Didn't I say, 'What profit would there be for one to gain the whole world and forfeit his life?'" (Matt. 16:26) Nor can you plead that the devil tempted you. Remember, God didn't excuse Eve when she pleaded that the devil tempted her.

Knowing this awaits you will help you give glory to God before your final sunset. Better to let your tongue parch from privation and fasting during the short space of this life than to expose yourself to eternal thirst via sinful indulgences.

Hopefully, the contemplation of this terrible truth will remove your indifference and motivate you to practice virtue. Do works of charity, justice, and salvation. Confess your sins and do penances. Amend your life, for God will give eternal life to those who labor courageously and profitably, and eternal death to those who pursue barren and useless things.

Chapter 9

The Ninth Motive for practicing Virtue: The Thought of Heaven

The reward of Heaven provides an equally powerful motive to pursue a virtuous life. Heaven, a place of supreme excellence and beauty, more importantly has the perfection and beauty of our Sovereign King who reigns there with His elect.

Obviously, no one can fully express the splendor and riches of Heaven, but we do have some limited insight into its magnificence. Consider the infinite power and boundless riches of God Himself. With His immense power, He needed only a single word to create the universe, and with a single word, He could reduce it to nothingness. A single expression of His will would suffice to create millions of worlds as beautiful as ours, or to destroy them in an instant.

Moreover, He exercises His power effortlessly. With equal ease, He creates the most sublime Seraphim or the smallest insect. He accomplishes all through His will. Because His power is so great, we know that the splendor and magnificence of His Heaven soars beyond our earthly ability to comprehend. Heaven contains perfection in all aspects because all riches, all power, and all wisdom come from God. In all its beauty, heaven combines the almighty power of the Father, the infinite wisdom of the Son, and the inexhaustible goodness of the Holy Spirit.

How amazing that God has prepared this magnificence not only for His glory, but for ours as well, for scripture says, "I will honor those who honor me, but those who spurn me shall be accursed." (1Sam. 2:30)

You can catch a faint glimpse of the nobility and grandeur of Heaven, which Scripture calls the land of the living, by comparing it to your present existence that you can truly call the land of the dying. However, even our imperfect world contains great beauty and perfection. It has beautiful blue skies, the dazzling splendor of the sun, the soft radiance of the moon and stars, the green beauty of the earth, the rich colors of the birds, the grandeur of the mountains, the sparkling freshness of streams, the majesty of great rivers, the vastness of the seas, the beauty of deep lakes, and flower-filled fields. If we find such beauty in this land of death, imagine the spectacle that waits in the haven of eternal rest.

Heaven contains another glory incomparably superior to anything on earth: the vision and possession of God Himself. St. Augustine said that the reward of virtue is God Himself, whom you will untiringly contemplate, love, and praise for all eternity. (City of God, 22, 30) The blessed inhabitants of Heaven enjoy in Him all good. Because God creates every good, it follows that He possesses in Himself all perfection and all goodness in an infinite degree.

God will be the fulfillment of all your desires. In Him, you'll find perfection and enjoy the balmy freshness of spring, the rich beauty of summer, the luxurious abundance of autumn, and the calm repose of winter. St. Bernard said,

"God will fill our understanding with the plenitude of light, our wills with an abundance of peace, and our memories with the joys of eternity."

Amazingly, knowing all this, many seek vain and sensual satisfactions from the world. If you crave joy, contemplate the Good that contains all joy. If you seek beauty, live so that one day you may possess the source of all beauty. If you find happiness in friendship and the society of generous hearts, consider the noble beings who wait to befriend you for eternity. If you seek wealth and honor, seek the treasures and the glory of Heaven. Finally, if you desire freedom from all evil and rest from all labor, know that Heaven alone can satisfy your desires. Knowing all these things, don't be too stubborn and prideful to live a life of virtue.

Chapter 10

The Tenth Motive for practicing Virtue:
The Thought of Hell

A sinner can't find comfort by saying, "The only result of my depravity means I will never see God. Beyond this, I won't have any reward or punishment." Scripture teaches the fallacy of this in Jeremiah 24:1-2. Here, in a vision, Jeremiah saw happiness and misery represented by two baskets of figs. One contained very good figs and the other very bad, inedible figs. These baskets represented two classes of souls, one the object of God's mercy, the other of His justice. The happiness of the first knows no limit and the misery of the second, unimaginable.

Don't sin rashly and weigh the truth of the terrible burden that you lay upon yourself if you do. A Doctor of the Church says that if you shed one tear every thousand years and they accumulated to a flood that inundated the world, you'd remain as far as ever from the end of your sufferings.

Perhaps God would forgive your sins if you didn't know these infallible truths. But we received them from Jesus when He said, "Heaven and earth will pass away, but my words will not pass away." (Lk. 21:33)

Chapter 11

The Eleventh Motive for practicing Virtue: The Inestimable Advantages Promised in this Life

With such powerful reasons for embracing virtue, I don't know any excuse to avoid its practice. Nevertheless, Christians continue to live wedded to the things of this world, ignoring God as if death and judgment or Heaven and Hell didn't exist. Many people do this because they believe they can't gain any advantage from virtue in this life and that its rewards belong to the next life.

Self-interest provides a very powerful motivator for most people and present circumstances make such strong impressions that they think very little of future rewards and seek only immediate satisfaction. The same held true in the days of the prophets. When Ezekiel made any promise or uttered any threat in the name of the Lord, people laughed at him and said to one another, "The vision he sees is a long way off; he prophesies of the distant future!" (Ezech. 12:27)

Because the wicked often prosper, many conclude that the labor of virtue is all in vain. St. Ambrose described people like this by saying, "They find it too difficult to buy hopes at the cost of dangers, to sacrifice present pleasures to future blessings." To destroy this serious error I know nothing better than the touching words of Our Savior weeping over Jerusalem: "If this day you only knew what makes for peace—but now it is hidden from your eyes." (Lk. 19:42)

When Jesus came in meekness and humility, He brought advantages and happiness but many coldly rejected Him. He shed bitter tears over this and foretold their unhappy fates. Jesus revealed this when Peter asked Him what reward they'd receive for leaving everything for love of Him. He said, "Amen, I say to you, there is no one who has given up house or brothers or sisters or mother or father or children or lands for my sake and for the sake of the gospel who will not receive a hundred times more now in this present age..." (Mk. 10:29-30) Notice how explicitly Jesus distinguished the rewards of this life and of the next.

What about this hundredfold that the just receive in this life? They aren't honors, riches, titles, and dignities. Most people of virtue lead hidden, obscure lives, forgotten by the world and overwhelmed with infirmities. So how does God fulfill His promise to give them a hundredfold in this life? He does it by blessing them with joy, peace, and happiness. Most people don't know these blessings, nor can they buy them with their wealth.

Study the lives of the saints and you'll learn they received the hundredfold promised in this life. In exchange for the false riches they forsook, they received true riches that they carry with them for eternity. For the turmoil and conflicts of the world, they received "peace which surpassed all understanding." Their tears, their fasting, and their prayers brought them more joy and consolation than they could ever obtain from the fleeting pleasures of this life.

If you can forsake your earthly father for love of God, your Heavenly Father will receive you as His child and make you His heir to everlasting inheritance. If you despise earthly pleasures for love of Him, He'll fill you with the sweetness of heavenly consolations. He'll open the eyes of your soul and you'll love and cherish what formerly frightened you. Bitterness will become sweetness and enlightened by grace, you'll see the emptiness of worldly joys, and you'll learn to relish the delights of God's love.

The annals of the Cistercian Order mention Arnulph, a man of prominence in Flanders strongly wedded to the things of this world, who converted to Catholicism after hearing St. Bernard preach. God filled him with so much grace that he became a Cistercian monk. One day he fell dangerously ill and remained unconscious for some time. The monks, believing him near death, administered the Sacrament of Healing. Soon after, his consciousness returned and he started yelling and frequently repeating, "How true are Thy words, oh merciful Jesus!" To questions he repeated, "How true are Thy words, oh merciful Jesus!" Some of them remarked that pain had made him delirious. "No, my brothers," he exclaimed. "I'm conscious and in full possession of my senses, and again I assure you that all the words Jesus has uttered are true."

"We don't doubt this," said the monks. "Why do you repeat it so often?"

He answered, "God says in the Gospel that he who forsakes earthly affections for love of Him shall receive a hundredfold in this world, and in the world to come, life everlasting, and I have already experienced the truth of His promise. Great as my present pains are, I would not exchange them with the anticipation of heavenly sweetness that they've procured me. If a guilty sinner like me receives such sweetness and consolation in the midst of his pains, what must be the joys of perfect souls?" The monks marveled to hear a man of no learning speak so wisely, but recognized in his words the inspiration of the Holy Spirit.

Therefore, the just, though deprived of earthly blessings, enjoy the rewards promised to virtue in this life. To convince you more fully, the next twelve chapters focus on the privileges attached to virtue in this world.

Chapter 12

The First Privilege of Virtue:
God's fatherly Care of the Just

God exercises the greatest care over those who serve Him virtuously. To appreciate this you must experience it, or study Holy Scripture that shows God's care for all His creatures. Throughout the Bible, God promises wondrous rewards for obeying Him and severe torments for those who don't. All the moral books contain God's commands, promises and threats, while the historical books record their fulfillment.

The most important of these blessings is His fatherly love and care for you that exceeds that of any earthly father. No earthly father can provide an inheritance of eternal glory or has ever suffered for his children the torments endured by Jesus that purchased the Kingdom of Heaven with the last drop of His Blood. Nothing surpasses His constant care for you as you remain always in His mind, while He helps and supports you in all you do.

Besides this, "...God commands the angels to guard you in all your ways." Thus, these pure spirits help the just to walk in the way of piety. Nor does their ministry cease at death, for Luke taught that angels carried the holy beggar Lazarus to Abraham's bosom.

This protection delivers the just from evil and leads them to good, and turns their sins to profit. For after a fall they acquire greater prudence, greater humility, and love God more tenderly for pardoning their offenses and delivering them from their evils. Hence, the Apostle said, "We know that all things work for good for those who love God, who are called according to his purpose." (Rom. 8:28)

If God's love for you leaves you unmoved, at least consider how He punishes the wicked. Scripture says, "I will hide my face from them and see what will then become of them. What a fickle race they are, sons with no loyalty in them!" (Deut. 32:20)

No greater misfortune exists than for God to remove His care in a world filled with dangers and numerous enemies. How terrible to have no one to help you to avoid their snares. Without divine assistance, you can't avoid destruction.

But the punishment of the wicked doesn't end here. God abandons them to their weakness and scourges them with His justice, so that the eyes which before watched for their happiness now look unmoved upon their ruin. This God Himself says by the mouth of the prophet, "Though they are led into captivity by their enemies, there will I command the sword to slay them. I will fix my gaze upon them for evil, and not for good." (Amos 9:4) Who can read these words of God, and not tremble at the misfortune of having an enemy so powerful and so relentless in seeking his destruction?

Behold, dear Christian, how God's providence surrounds you. If a sense of gratitude for His paternal care doesn't motivate you to serve Him, at least let the fear of His abandonment impel you.

Chapter 13

The Second Privilege of Virtue:
The Grace with which the Holy Spirit
Fills Devout Souls

God, through His fatherly providence, provides all favors and privileges to those who serve Him so they can achieve perfection and happiness. The most important of these, the grace of the Holy Spirit, provides the source of all other heavenly gifts. God's grace lessens your corrupt nature, clothes you in the beauty and nobility of Jesus Christ, and allows you to participate in His sanctity, purity, and greatness.

Holy writers illustrate this with a familiar example. A piece of iron, when taken out of the fire, remains iron, but it glows with heat and brightness. Grace acts in a similar way. As divine grace fills you with virtues and the purity of God, your soul glows but you remain human. The Apostle Paul described this change when he said, "Yet I live, no longer but Christ lives in me..." (Gal. 2:20)

Grace also appears as a beautiful spiritual dress for the soul, that makes your soul so beautiful that God adopts it as His child, or takes it as His spouse. This realization made the prophet Isaiah rejoice and say, "I rejoice heartily in the Lord, in my God is the joy of my soul; for he has clothed me with a robe of salvation, and wrapped me in a mantle of justice; like a bridegroom adorned with a diadem, like a bride bedecked with her jewels." (Is. 61:10)

Grace makes you so pleasing to God that your good actions earn merits for eternal life. By good actions, I mean both acts of virtue and the necessities of nature, such as eating, drinking, and sleeping. When performed with upright intentions, these ordinary tasks please God and earn merit.

Grace smoothes the way to Heaven; makes the yoke of Christ sweet and light; cures your infirmities; and lightens your burdens so you can run in the path of virtue. Grace strengthens all the faculties of the soul; enlightens the understanding; inflames the heart; moderates the appetites of the flesh; and constantly stimulates you so you can't relax in the pursuit of virtue. Likewise, it provides sentinels to guard the inferior parts of your soul through which the enemy attempts to gain entrance, and fills you with virtues that have the opposite nature of temptations. Thus, temperance resists gluttony, chastity combats impurity, and humility overcomes pride. Ultimately, grace brings God into your soul to govern you, protect you, and lead you to Heaven. Knowing this, never turn away from God.

Chapter 14

The Third Privilege of Virtue:
The Supernatural Light and Knowledge
Granted to Virtuous Souls

Heavenly light and wisdom combine to form the third reward of virtue. They moderate your appetites; strengthen your will; remove the darkness of sin from your understanding; and help you know and fulfill your duty.

St. Gregory taught that sin brings the punishments of ignorance of your duty, and the inability to do your duty. (Moral. L. 25, c. 9) God, by His grace, teaches what things to desire and provides the strength to do them.

Four of these gifts relate to understanding. Wisdom instructs us in spiritual things. Knowledge provides basic data. Understanding helps us to appreciate the beauty of divine mysteries. Finally, counsel guides us through the difficulties in the pursuit of virtue.

Because grace makes you virtuous, you love virtue and abhor sin. God helps you discern the malice of sin and the beauty of virtue because God provides all of creation everything necessary to survive. To name a few, He gives wild animals the ability to distinguish poisonous plants, build their homes, and migrate. If God gives animals these survival graces, believe that He has given you the knowledge necessary for the maintenance of your spiritual life.

Great differences exist between Divinely communicated knowledge and the knowledge you acquire in school. School knowledge only illumines the intellect, but Divine knowledge helps you discern inspirations from the Holy Spirit. Divine knowledge penetrates into the depths of your soul, transforms your passions, and remakes you in the likeness of Christ. Hence, the Apostle Paul taught, "Indeed, the word of God is living and effective, sharper than any two-edged sword, penetrating even between soul and spirit, joints and marrow, and able to discern reflections and thoughts of the heart." (Heb. 4:12)

Undeniable passages from the Old and New Testaments prove this truth to those reluctant to accept it. Our Savior says, "The Advocate, the Holy Spirit that the Father will send in my name, will teach you everything and remind you of all that I told you." (Jn. 14:26) And, "It is written in the prophets: 'They shall all be taught by God.' Everyone who listens to my Father and learns from Him comes to Me." (Jn. 6:45)

God also fills the souls of the just with brightness. He shows them the beauty of virtue and the deformity of vice. He reveals the vanity of this world, the treasures of grace, the greatness of eternal glory, and the sweetness of the consolations of the Holy Spirit. He teaches of the goodness of God, the malice of the evil one, the shortness of life, and the fatal error of those who focus on the things of this world. When God blesses you with this grace, you don't love prosperity or get depressed by adversity. Solomon said, "Ever wise are the discourses of the devout, but the godless man, like the moon, is inconstant." (Sir. 27:11) Unmoved by the winds of false doctrine, the just man continues steadfast in

Christ, immovable in charity, unswerving in faith.

Let me close with a final note of caution. Even though God can fill the souls of the just with His wisdom, no person, no matter how great the gift, can lawfully refuse to follow the direction of their legitimate superiors, especially authorized teachers and leaders of the Church. No one ever received greater light than St. Paul, who God raised to the third heaven, or than Moses, who spoke face to face with God. Yet St. Paul went to Jerusalem to confer with the Apostles about the Gospel that he received from Christ Himself, and Moses did not disdain to accept the advice of his father-in-law, a Gentile.

Always remember, the interior gifts of grace don't exclude the exterior succors of the Church. As the sun warms your body while at the same time you generate your own warmth, the light of grace glows brighter with the teaching and guidance of the Church. Therefore, whoever fills with pride and refuses to submit to her authority becomes unworthy of God's favors.

Chapter 15

The Fourth Privilege of Virtue: The Consolations with which the Holy Spirit visits the Just

No earthly pleasure compares to joy. When the power of joy overcame St. Ephrem he'd cry out, "Withdraw from me a little, oh Lord, for my body faints under the weight of your delights!" In this inebriation of heavenly sweetness, you'll forget the troubles and trials of the world and your soul will soar to joys beyond the power of your natural faculties.

You'll probably tell me that God reserves these consolations for those advanced in virtue. Yes, more perfect souls know more of these intimate joys, yet the Divine Master even grants beginners ineffable rewards. You provide no argument against this truth when you say that you don't experience these Divine consolations when you think of God. Food remains tasteless to a disordered palate, and for a soul filled with sin, this heavenly manna has no relish.

Dear Christian, don't delay! Every moment contains more value to you than all the riches of the universe. And if you attain this heavenly treasure, you'll never cease to lament the time you lost, and to cry out with St. Augustine, "Too late have I known You, too late I loved You, oh beauty ever ancient and ever new!" St. Augustine, though he always lamented the lateness of his conversion, gave himself to God with all his heart and won an immortal crown. Imitate him, and avoid the unhappiness of lamenting the delay of your conversion and the loss of your crown.

Chapter 16

The Fifth Privilege of Virtue:
The Peace of a Good Conscience

God places great value on another one of His gifts, your conscience. He placed this unsleeping guardian in the center of your soul that never ceases to guide and sustain you. Epictetus taught this truth when he said, "As fathers entrust their children to a tutor who will prudently guard them from vice and lead them to virtue, so God entrusts you to the care of that interior guide which stimulates you to virtue and warns against vice."

Conscience, always a kind master to the just, scourges the wicked. It tortures them with the remembrance of their crimes and embitters all their illicit pleasures.

Virtue shelters you from remorse and sufferings. The consolations and sweet fruits of the Holy Spirit can fill you with joy and transform your soul into a terrestrial paradise. St. Augustine said, "The joy of a good conscience makes the soul a true paradise." (De Gen. ad Lit., L. 12, c. 34)

God gave you everything you need to achieve perfection. He endowed you with natural inclinations for good and an instinctive hatred of evil. Sin may weaken it, but it never destroys it.

Chapter 17

The Sixth Privilege of Virtue:
The Confidence of the Just

"The blessed gift of rejoicing in patience during tribulations always accompanies the joy of a good conscience." (Rom. 12:12) God gives you this rich inheritance as a refuge in tribulation and your best remedy against the miseries of life.

Faith comes in two forms, dead and living. Living faith gains strength through charitable acts. Hope also comes in two forms, barren and lively. Barren hope provides no light, strength, or consolation during difficult times. Lively hope consoles you in sorrow, strengthens you in labor, and sustains you in dangers and trials.

Lively hope works many marvelous effects in your soul which increase with charitable acts, and provides the strength to accomplish the labors of life by holding before your eyes your eternal reward. The stronger the hope of reward, the greater your courage to overcome obstacles in the path of virtue.

St. Gregory taught, "Hope focuses your hearts so steadfastly upon the joys of Heaven that you remain insensible to the miseries of life." St. Chrysostom said, "If the furious tempests of the sea can't deter the sailor, if hard frosts and withering blight can't discourage the farmer, if neither wounds nor death frighten the soldier, how much greater the courage of a Christian who toils for eternal reward!" Don't focus on the roughness of the path of virtue, but rather its destination. And don't admire the pleasures adorning the path of vice, rather upon the cliff it leads to.

In the inestimable treasures of hope, we have some idea of the blessings the wicked don't have. Their sins kill their hope, and distrust and fear follow them like their own shadows. Hence, sinners find only fleeting happiness when they pursue the vanities and follies of this world.

No misery compares to life without hope. When you live without hope, you live without God. No nation, however barbarous, exists without some knowledge of God and thus they have hope. When Moses left the children of Israel for a short time, they imagined themselves without God and in their ignorance, they asked Aaron to give them a God, for they feared to continue without one. Thus, human nature, though ignorant of the true God, instinctively acknowledges the necessity of a supreme being.

As ivy clings to a tree, and as spouses depend on each other, we seek the protection and assistance of God. Those who deprive themselves of His support live in a deplorable condition. They have no one to turn to for comfort in trials, relief in sickness, protection in dangers, or counsel in difficulties.

Behold, then, dear Christian, God's great gift of hope, which proceeds from His goodness and His paternal providence. Knowing of His fatherly care strengthens your confidence and energizes your hope.

Chapter 18

The Seventh Privilege of Virtue: The True Liberty of the Just

From these privileges, and particularly from the graces of the Holy Spirit, arises a seventh marvelous privilege, true liberty of the soul. As your Redeemer, Jesus brought this gift to you. He freed you from the slavery of sin and restored you to the true liberty of the children of God. This is one of the greatest of God's favors, one of the most beautiful benefits of the Gospel, and one of the principal effects of the Holy Spirit. "Now the Lord is the Spirit, and where the Spirit of the Lord is, there is freedom." (2Cor. 3:17) This liberty is one of the most magnificent rewards that God has promised to His servants in this life. "…If you remain in my word, you will truly be my disciples, and you will know the truth, and the truth will set you free." (Jn 8:31-32)

Our Savior teaches about two kinds of liberty, the liberty of the body and true liberty. You have liberty of the body when you give free reign to your bodily desires but sin enslaves your soul. True liberty rests with those free from sin even if chains and bars confine their bodies. Witness the great Apostle Paul, whose mind, despite his fetters, soared to Heaven, and whose preaching and doctrine freed the world.

To this, we unhesitatingly give the glorious name Liberty. For the soul provides your nobility and constitutes your being. Hence, a soul in a state of Liberty remains truly free, and a soul bound by sin, no matter how free the body, possesses only the semblance of Liberty.

Thus sin, the most cruel tyrant, binds the sinner. Since the torments of Hell result from sin, consider then the horribleness of sin itself. Jesus said that this cruel tyrant enslaves the wicked and "...everyone who commits sin is a slave of sin." (Jn. 8:34) Sin, the world via the devil, and the flesh enslave sinners. Together they imprison the soul and surrender it to a pitiless master.

The devil makes use of the flesh to tempt and incite you to every kind of iniquity. Therefore, the Apostle calls flesh "sin," giving the name of the effect to the cause, for flesh incites men to all evil. (Rom. 7:25) We refer to it as sensuality or concupiscence. St. Basil taught that the devil uses your desires as the main weapon to make war upon you. For carried away by the immoderate desires of the flesh, you seek to gratify them by any means in your power, regardless of God's law. From this disorder, all sins arise.

St. Paul taught that this appetite of the flesh makes a sinner a slave. However, at no time do sinners lose their free will, as you can never lose your free will no matter how many sins you commit. However, sin so weakens the will and so strengthens the appetites of the flesh, that the stronger naturally prevails over the weaker.

You possess a soul made in the image of God and a mind capable of rising above creatures to the contemplation of God. Yet many despise all these privileges and place themselves in subjection to the base appetites of a flesh corrupted by sin and incited and directed by the devil. You

58

can only expect innumerable falls and incomparable misfortunes from such choices.

Theologians say that souls consist of two parts, the superior and the inferior. God endowed you with the superior part as the home for your will and reason. This noble and beautiful gift enables you to enjoy God and raises you to a companionship with the angels. The inferior part of the soul provides the home for your sensual appetites, which God provided to help us procure the necessities of life and to preserve the human race. Reason must control these appetites, but often it is the other way around.

Such appetites enslave billions of people who transgress every law of justice and reason to gratify their sensual desires. Many carry the folly still further and make the noble faculty of reason serve their base appetites and furnish them with means to attain their unlawful desires. When you devote yourself to surpassing your neighbor in wealth and voluptuous luxuries, you turn your soul from noble and spiritual duties and make yourself a slave of the flesh. Seneca, though a pagan, blushed at such degradation, saying, "I was born for nobler things than to be a slave to the flesh." (Epist. 65) Notwithstanding the folly and enormity of this disorder, it is so common that we give it little attention. As St. Bernard said, "We are insensible to the odor of our crimes because they are so numerous."

Consider, for instance, all that a married person risks by pursuing a love affair. This person knows that if discovered, their spouse might fly into a rage and kill in anger. Thus, in one moment they could lose their reputation, children, life, and soul. Yet so great does their passion rage, that they trample all other considerations to obey its demands.

The wicked choose to live in such bondage. They sit "in

darkness and the shadow of death," says the prophet, "hungry and bound with chains." (Ps. 106:10) This darkness blinds them and they neither know themselves nor God, nor the end for which He created them. They don't see the vanity of the things upon which they set their hearts, and they remain insensible to the bondage in which they live.

Vice reduces people to slavery. Study someone who falls victim to pride or ambition and see how eagerly they grasp at honors, how they make them the end of all their actions. Their house, dress, and even their demeanor all fuse to excite the applause of the world. They constantly strive to win admiration with their words and actions. How astonishing and pitiable to see someone devote their life to pursuing worldly vanities that can end only in smoke. They enslave themselves and can't do their own will, can't dress to please themselves, can't go where they choose. They don't dare enter a church or talk with virtuous souls for fear their master, the world, will ridicule them.

To satisfy their ambitions they impose upon themselves innumerable privations. They live above their incomes, rob their children of their inheritances, and leave them only the burden of their debts and the evil example of their follies.

Jesus delivered you from this miserable slavery. He redeemed you by His superabundant grace. He purchased you by His sacrifice on the cross. Hence, the Apostle says, "We know that our old self was crucified with Him, so that our sinful body might be done away with, that we might no longer be in slavery to sin." (Rom. 6:6) By the merits of His crucifixion, He strengthened you with grace, so that the spirit rules the flesh and makes it the docile instrument of the noblest deeds. His grace nourishes your virtues, subdues your passions, and compels you to submit to reason. Grace so charms your passions that though they continue to exist in your nature, they can no longer harm you with their poison.

The just also experience the joy of a good conscience and spiritual consolations. These so satisfy one's thirst for happiness that one can easily resist the grosser pleasures of the flesh. Having found the fountain of all happiness, such people desire no other pleasures.

St. Gregory developed this line of thought when he said that when someone experiences the sweetness of the spiritual life, they reject the objects of sensual love. He generously disposes of his treasures as his heart inflames with a desire for heavenly things. He sees deformity in the beauty that formerly allured them. His heart overflows with the water of life and, therefore, he has no thirst for the fleeting pleasures of the world. He finds the Lord in all things and He becomes the master of all things, for this one Good contains every other good.

The just also regain their liberty via their unceasing labors to bring the flesh under the dominion of reason. They gradually moderate their passions that formerly attacked their soul. Habit does much to cause this happy change, but grace aids and confirms their wonderful effort.

Hence those who serve God very often find more pleasure in recollection, silence, pious reading, meditation, prayer, and other devout exercises than in any worldly amusement. Don't let the ease with which you win these victories disarm your prudence or render you less vigilant in guarding the senses as long as you live.

Chapter 19

The Eighth Privilege of Virtue:
The Peace Enjoyed by the Just

The just enjoy interior peace and tranquility. To understand this more clearly, focus on the three kinds of peace: peace with God, peace with your neighbor, and peace with yourself.

Peace with God consists in the favor and friendship of God. St. Paul described it as, "Therefore, since we have been justified by faith, we have peace with God through our Lord Jesus Christ." (Rom. 5:1) Peace with your neighbors consists in a friendly union that banishes all ill will toward them. To this peace, St. Paul exhorted the Romans, "If possible, on your part, live at peace with all." (Rom. 12:18) Peace with yourself comes from a good conscience and the harmony existing between the spirit and the flesh when the laws of reason triumph over the desires of the flesh.

The just also enjoy liberty gained by the triumph of the nobler part of the soul over their inferior appetites. Great spiritual consolations form another source of this peace. They soothe the affections and appetites of the flesh by making them content to share in the joys of the spirit, which they relish, as they better understand the sovereign sweetness of

God. Seeking no other delights, they never find disappointment, and consequently never feel the attacks of anger. Peace reigns in their souls.

Finally, the just have the ultimate confidence in God even during trials and storms. They know that God is their Father, Defender, and Shield. Hence, they can say with the prophet, "In peace I shall both lie down and sleep, for you alone, Lord, make me secure." (Ps. 4:9)

Chapter 20

The Ninth Privilege of Virtue: The Manner in which God Hears the Prayers of the Just

Two universal deluges, one material, the other moral, covered the earth. The former took place in the time of Noah and destroyed everything but the ark and its contents. The moral deluge, much worse than the material, rose from the sin of our first parents. That original sin affected our souls more than our bodies, for it robbed us of all the spiritual riches and supernatural treasures God bestowed upon us through Adam and Eve.

From this first deluge came all the miseries under which we groan. So great and so numerous are these that Pope Innocent III devoted an entire work to them. (Innocent III, *De Vilitate Conditionis Humanae*)

Philosophers considering on the one hand our superiority to all other creatures, and on the other the miseries and vices that assault us, have greatly wondered at such contradictions in so noble a creature. Unenlightened by revelation, they didn't understand the cause of this discord. They saw that of all animals, we have the most infirmities of body and that ambition and avarice torment only people. Only humans seek to prolong their lives and have strange anxieties concerning burials. Stranger yet, we have an anxiety about our condition after death. They recognized that we suffer innumerable accidents and miseries. Finally, we must earn our bread by the sweat of our brow.

Reduced to this miserable condition and deprived of our possessions by the first deluge, God provided the remedy of turning to Him and crying out, "…We are at a loss what to do, hence our eyes are turned toward you." (2Chron 20:12) Thus, when all other avenues of hope close and all other resources fail, turn to prayer, the sovereign remedy for every evil.

You'll ask, perhaps, whether this truly provides a remedy for every evil. As this depends solely upon the will of God, the Apostles and prophets alone can answer because God instructed them in the secret of His will. "For what great nation is there that has gods so close to it as the Lord, our God, is to us whenever we call upon Him?" (Deut. 4:7) These words of God Himself assure with absolute certainty that you don't pray in vain. God, always invisibly present, receives every sigh of your soul with compassion and grants what you ask, if for your good. He says, "Ask and it will be given to you; seek and you will find; knock and the door will be opened to you." (Matt. 7:7) What stronger, what fuller pledge can you find to allay your doubts?

To learn how God fulfills such promises, study the lives of the saints and see what marvels they effected by prayer. See what Moses accomplished by prayer in Egypt and throughout the journey of the Israelites in the desert. Learn about the wonderful works of Elias and his disciple Eliseus. Behold the miracles of the Apostles. Moreover, the saints used this weapon to overcome the world. By prayer, they ruled the elements and converted fierce flames into refreshing dew. By prayer, they disarmed the wrath of God and opened the fountains of His mercy. By prayer, they obtained all their desires.

St. Dominic once told a friend that he never failed to obtain a favor asked of God. Whereupon his friend asked him to pray that a celebrated doctor named Reginald might become a member of his order. The saint spent the night in prayer for this disciple and early in the morning, as he began the first hymn of the morning office, Reginald suddenly came into the choir, prostrated himself at the feet of the saint, and begged for the habit of his order. God rewards the obedience of the just who willingly listen to His commandments by attentively hearing their supplications.

However, God answers the prayers of the wicked very differently. "When you spread out your hands, I close my eyes to you. Though you pray the more, I will not listen. Your hands are full of blood!" (Is. 1:15)

Nevertheless, the sinner who reads these lines shouldn't get discouraged. God only rejects the obstinately wicked. He cuts them off only if they wish to continue their disorders. Though you have sins as numerous as the sands on the beach, never forget that God is your Father. He awaits you with open arms and an open heart and He continually calls you to return and reconcile to Him. Have the desire to change your life and resolve to walk in the path of virtue. Turn to God in humble prayer with unshaken confidence that He'll hear you. "Ask, and you shall receive; seek, and you shall find; knock, and it shall be opened to you."

Chapter 21

The Tenth Privilege of Virtue:
The Consolation and Assistance with which
God sustains the Just in their Afflictions

No one's happiness rests secure from the danger of accidents and misfortunes. However, the just and the wicked act quite differently under tribulation. The just know God as their Father and the physician of their souls, and submissively and generously accept the bitter chalice of suffering as the cure for their infirmities. They look on tribulation as a file in the hands of their Maker to remove the rust of sin from their soul. They know affliction makes them more humble, increases the fervor of their prayers, and purifies their conscience.

Now no physician more carefully proportions his remedies to the strength of his patient than this Heavenly Physician tempers trials according to the necessities of souls. If their burdens increase, He redoubles the measure of their consolations. Seeing the riches they acquire by sufferings, the just no longer fly from them, but eagerly desire them and meet them with patience and even joy. They don't focus on the bitter medicine, but on how it will restore their health. They trust in a God who chastises those He loves. (Heb. 12:6)

The just never lack grace of fortitude in time of tribulation. Though He seems to have withdrawn from them, God remains closer to His children during these times. Search Scriptures and you'll see this thought frequently repeated. For example, in the Psalms we read, "Then call on me in time of distress, I will rescue you, and you shall honor me." (Ps. 49:15)

However, consider the unfortunate condition of the wicked when afflicted. Devoid of hope, of charity, of courage, of every sustaining virtue, tribulation attacks them unarmed and defenseless. Their dead faith sheds no ray of light on the darkness of their afflictions. Hope holds out no future reward to sustain their failing courage. Utterly defenseless, they can't swim in the angry waves dashing them to pieces against the rocks of pride, despair, rage, and blasphemy.

Observe the extravagant grief of the wicked when those they love die. They storm against Heaven and deny God's justice. They blaspheme God, rage against others and sometimes end their miserable lives by their own hands. Their curses and blasphemies bring upon them terrible calamities, for Divine Justice punishes those who rebel against the providence of God.

Unhappy souls! The afflictions God sends to cure their disorders only increase their misery. The pains of Hell begin for them in this world. About this St. Chrysostom taught, "The same fire that purifies gold, consumes wood; so in the fire of tribulation the just acquire new beauty and perfection, while the wicked, like dry wood, reduce to ashes." (Hom.14 in Matt.1)

Chapter 22

The Eleventh Privilege of Virtue:
God's Care for the Temporal Needs of the Just

The Wise Man said of wisdom, "Long life is in her right hand, in her left are riches and honor." (Prov. 3:16) Perfect virtue offers both temporal blessings of this life and eternal blessings of heaven. God doesn't leave His followers in want. He carefully provides for the smallest of His creatures, and doesn't disregard the necessities of His faithful servants.

Don't accept this on my word, rather read St. Matthew's Gospel and you'll find many assurances and promises on this subject. "Look at the birds in the sky; they do not sow or reap, they gather nothing into barns, yet your heavenly Father feeds them. Are not you more important than they? So do not worry and say, 'What are we to eat?' or 'What are we to drink?' or 'What are we to wear?' All these things the pagans seek. Your heavenly Father knows that you need them all. But seek first the kingdom (of God) and his righteousness, and all these things will be given you besides." (Matt. 6:26, 31-33)

No riches compare to such blessings as these. Moreover, God bestows them with two extraordinary advantages unknown to the wicked. First, God bestows them with wisdom. Like a skillful physician, He gives His servants temporal blessings according to their necessities, and not in such measure as to inflate them with pride or endanger their salvation. The wicked despise this moderation and madly heap up all the riches they can acquire, forgetting that excess endangers the soul just like too much food injures the body.

Secondly, these blessings provide the just with the rest and contentment everyone seeks in worldly goods. Even with a little, the just enjoy as much repose as if they possessed the universe. Hence, St. Paul speaks of himself as having nothing, yet possessing all things. (2Cor. 6:10) Thus the just journey through life poor, but knowing no want, and possessing abundance in the midst of poverty. The wicked, on the contrary, hunger in the midst of abundance and though surrounded by water, they can never satisfy their thirst.

Therefore, virtue helps attain the joys of eternity and secure the blessings of this life. Let it renew your ardor in the practice of virtue, which can save you from so many miseries and procure you so many blessings.

Chapter 23

The Twelfth Privilege of Virtue:
The Happy Death of the Just

God crowns the just man most fittingly in death. Moreover, He provides the departing sinner with a fitting close to his wretched career. "Too costly in the eyes of the Lord is the death of his faithful," (Ps.116:15) says the Psalmist, but "evil will slay the wicked; those who hate the just are condemned." (Ps. 34:22) Commenting upon the death of sinners, St. Bernard said that the death of the wicked is bad because it takes them from this world, separates the soul from the body, sends them into the fires of Hell, and makes them prey to the undying worm of remorse.

To these evils, which haunt sinners at the hour of death, add the bitter regrets that gnaw their hearts, the anguish that fills their souls, and the torments that rack their bodies. Terrors seize them with thoughts of the past, the account they must render, and the sentence God will pronounce against them. They fret about the horrors of the tomb, the separation from family and friends, and the bidding farewell to the things they've loved with an inordinate and a guilty love of wealth. The more they love earthly things, the more bitter their anguish at separating from them.

The greatest suffering of the wicked at the hour of death

comes from the stings of remorse and thoughts of their terrible future. St. Eusebius said that as life ebbs away, the necessities of life no longer provide distraction. You no longer desire honors for they move beyond your grasp. Eternal interests and thoughts of God's justice demand all attention. The past with its pleasures leaves and the present with its opportunities rapidly glides away. The future only remains with the dismal prospect of many sins waiting to accuse you before the judgment seat of our all-just God.

At the hour of death the wicked receive the punishment for their crimes, whereas the just receive the reward of their virtues. The Holy Spirit tells us, "He who fears the Lord will have a happy end; even on the day of his death he will be blessed." (Sir. 1:11) St. John declares this truth still more forcibly when he declared he heard a voice from Heaven commanding him, "Write: Blessed are the dead who die in the Lord from now on. Yes, let them find rest from their labors, for their works accompany them." (Rev. 14:13) With this promise from God, the just have nothing to fear.

St. Gregory said that the light that illumines the close of the just man's life reflects the splendor of immortal glory that draws near. St. Martin provides a striking example of this confident hope. Seeing the devil beside his bed at the hour of death, he cried out, "What are you doing here, cruel beast? You'll find no mortal sin in my soul to bind me. I go to enjoy eternal peace in Abraham's bosom."

St. Dominic had equally touching and beautiful confidence. Seeing the religious of his order weeping around his bed, he said to them, "Weep not, my children, for I can do you more good where I am going than I could ever hope to do on earth."

Far from fearing death, the just hail the hour of their

deliverance as the beginning of their reward. St. Augustine wrote that the just don't endure death with patience so they can be with Christ, but rather they endure life with patience and embrace death with joy. They don't fear death because they've always feared God. They prepared their whole life for it. During their lifetime they secured virtue and good works as powerful advocates for their final hour. Finally, they don't fear death because death provides only sweet sleep, the end of toil, and the beginning of blessed immortality.

Thus, we have seen the twelve fruits of virtue in this life, but many Christians make no effort to obtain this inestimable good. If a friend assured you that a treasure lay hidden in your house, you'd search for it, even if you doubted its existence. Yet though you know, on the infallible word of God, that you can find a priceless treasure within your own breast, you don't do anything to discover it. You forget the prodigal son and so many others who have returned from sin to their loving Father. You forget that when you do penance for your sins, God will forget your iniquities. (Ezech. 18:21-22)

Chapter 24

The Folly of Those who Defer their Conversion

Sinners never lack excuses to defend their loose lives. Scripture says, "The sinner turns aside reproof and distorts the law to suit his purpose." (Sir.32:17) Some defer salvation to an indefinite future, others until the hour of death. Many allege the task too difficult and arduous. Others presume upon God's mercy, persuaded that faith will save them without works of charity. Some, enslaved by the pleasures of the world, remain unwilling to sacrifice them for the happiness God promises. Satan uses all these snares to allure millions to sin, and he keeps them in bondage until death surprises them.

First, I will address those who defer conversion, alleging they can turn to God more effectively at another time. St. Augustine used this excuse to defer living a virtuous life saying, "Later, Lord, later I will abandon the world and sin." The father of lies uses this ruse to deceive the unwary. A Christian should desire salvation above all else. To obtain salvation, sinners must change their lives. Therefore, sinners must decide when this change will begin. They say, "At a future day."

I answer, "At this present moment." They urge that later

will be easier. I insist that it is easier now. Let's see who is right.

You can't really know you'll have the time in the future to amend your life. The devil deceives many with this false hope. St. Gregory says, "God promises to receive the repentant sinner when he returns to Him, but nowhere does He promise to give him tomorrow."

The number of souls lost in this way must number in the millions. It ruined the rich man in the Gospel, whose terrible history St. Luke related. "There was a rich man whose land produced a bountiful harvest. He asked himself, 'What shall I do, for I do not have space to store my harvest?' And he said, 'This is what I shall do: I shall tear down my barns and build larger ones. There I shall store all my grain and other goods and I shall say to myself, Now as for you, you have so many good things stored up for many years, rest, eat, drink, be merry!' But God said to him, 'You fool, this night your life will be demanded of you and the things you have prepared, to whom will they belong?' Thus will it be for the one who stores up treasure for himself but is not rich in what matters to God." (Lk. 12:16-21) What great folly to rely on the future, as if time belongs to you.

However, even if you live as long as you imagine, what would be easier, a conversion now or later? To make this point clear, consider the causes that make sincere conversion difficult. The tyranny of bad habits provides the first cause. Many would rather die than give them up. Hence, St. Jerome declared that a long habit of sin robs virtue of all sweetness because habit becomes second nature, and to overcome it you must conquer nature itself. St. Bernard taught that when habit confirms vice, one can't get rid of it except by very special miraculous grace.

When God sees your habit of sin, He withdraws further and further, for Sacred Scripture teaches, "Woe to them, they have strayed from me. Woe to them when I turn away from them." (Hosea 7:13 and 9:12)

Finally, the corruption of sin darkens understanding, excites the sensual appetites, and weakens the will; then troubles and disorders soon follow. You can't convert more easily in the future, since every day increases the obstacles you now dread and weakens your forces to combat them. If you can't ford the present stream, you'll definitely drown when it swells to an angry torrent. Perhaps you now harbor a dozen vices which you tremble to attack. Imagine the courage you'll need when they increase a hundredfold. If a year or two of sinful habits baffle you now, imagine their strength in ten years. Satan relied on this craftiness when he deceived our first parents, and he continually applies it to you.

Also, don't lose sight of the satisfaction God requires for sin which, in the opinion of St. John Climachus, you can only with great difficulty satisfy each day the faults you commit each day. Thus, it makes no sense to accumulate more debt of sin and defer its payment to old age. St. Gregory considered this the basest treason, and those who defer the duty of penance to old age fall far short of the allegiance they owe to God. They also have much reason to fear God's justice rather than His mercy upon which they so rashly presume.

In Ecclesiastes God exhorts us to serve Him in youth and not defer it until the infirmities of old age make it impossible. "Remember your Creator in the days of your youth, before the evil days come. And the years approach of which you will say 'I have no pleasure in them.'" (Eccles. 12:10)

Therefore, don't defer your repentance until old age, when virtue will seem a necessity rather than a choice, and your vices will have left you rather than you leaving them. The salvation of your soul depends upon you promptly and submissively obeying God's inspiration. Make haste and don't delay your answer until tomorrow, start today because a timely beginning lessens the difficulty.

Chapter 25

Of those who Defer their Conversion until the Hour of Death

This chapter addresses the very common mistake of making deathbed confessions. Some of this material may alarm and discourage weaker souls. However, the consequences of presumption prove fatal, for a greater number perish through false confidence than through excessive fear. Therefore, I warn you about this danger so you won't rush blindly to your ruin and your blood be upon me. Holy Scripture, interpreted by the Fathers and Doctors of the Church, remains the safest guide, so we'll first study their opinions. Afterwards, we'll learn what God teaches through His inspired writers.

First, bear in mind an undeniable principle which St. Augustine taught. God inspires true repentance when and where He wills. Hence, if the heart of the sinner, even at the hour of death, fills with true contrition, salvation occurs. Perfect conversions of this type remain rare and not likely successful for those who defer repentance until the hour of death. Moreover, if they obtain salvation, temporal punishment in Purgatory remains for their sins. Moreover, the fires of Purgatory cause greater suffering than any known on earth. Therefore, to avoid these dreadful punishments after death, begin now to amend your life.

St. Augustine, in *True and False Penance,* wrote that no one should hope to do penance when they can no longer sin. God wants you to repent cheerfully and not through compulsion. Therefore, if you wait to leave your sins until they leave you, you act from necessity rather than from choice.

If a person asked St. Ambrose for the sacrament of reconciliation as death neared, he didn't refuse it. However, he didn't dare to assure them that they'd go to Heaven. But if they did penance for their sins while healthy, he positively assured them they'd make their way to Heaven.

St. Gregory taught that God frequently inflicts punishment for sin even at the hour of death by allowing it to accompany the sinner to the tomb. We see striking proof of this when we see people unwilling to separate from the objects of their sinful life even at the last hour of death. By a just judgment of God, they expire completely forgetful of what they owe their Maker and their souls.

About this subject Holy Scripture warns, "Because I called and you refused, I extended my hand and no one took notice; because you disdained all my counsel, and my reproof you ignored—I, in my turn, will laugh at your doom; I will mock when terror overtakes you. Then they call me, but I answer not; they seek me, but find me not." (Prov. 1:24-26, 28)

In the New Testament, Jesus warns his Apostles of the day of His coming and of the need for readiness. He said, "Blessed is that servant whom his master on his arrival finds doing so. Amen, I say to you, he will put him in charge of all his property. But if that wicked servant says to himself, 'My master is long delayed,' and begins to beat his fellow servants and eat and drink with drunkards, the servant's master will come on an unexpected day and at an unknown hour and will punish him severely and assign him a place with the hypocrites, where there will be wailing and grinding of teeth." (Matt. 24:46-51)

I urge you, dear Christian, to think of the inevitable hour when you'll experience the truth of my predictions. You'll find yourself distracted with pain, filled with anguish and terror at the approach of death and at the thought of the eternal sentence Jesus will pronounce upon you. Vainly will you then try to change it to soften its rigor. However, what might fail then, you can easily accomplish now, because now you can make your sentence one filled with joy. Waste no time and hasten to soothe your Judge. On your day of judgment, you shall see Him, but He won't listen, unless you live so as to merit His blessings.

Chapter 26

Of Those who Continue in Sin, Trusting in the Mercy of God

Besides those who defer their conversion until the hour of death, others persevere in sin, trusting in the mercy of God and the merits of His Passion. I will disabuse them of this illusion.

Some say that God's mercy knows no bounds since He died on the cross for the salvation of sinners. What a strange teaching to think that because of God's goodness, you can sin with impunity. The Holy Spirit teaches no such thing. On the contrary, those who listen to His voice reason just the opposite. They say God is good; therefore, I must serve Him, obey Him, and love Him above all things. Thus, the more you rely on God's goodness, the more heinous your crimes against Him. God will punish these offenses and avenge your sins.

Many presume too much of God's mercy and show that they've never studied His justice. If they had, they'd cry out to the Lord with the psalmist, "Who comprehends your terrible anger? Your wrath matches the fear it inspires." (Ps. 90:11-12) Without the fear of God, the soul flounders like a ship without ballast and the winds of life sweep it to destruction. Even if richly laden with virtue, it remains in constant danger of crashing on the rocks of temptation. Therefore, both those who have just entered God's service and those who have long lived in His household carry this fear. The former because of their past transgressions, the latter because their weakness exposes them to danger at every moment.

Curiously, virtue causes virtue to increase and sin causes sin to increase. God chastises you when He permits you, through your blindness and passion, to rush headlong down the road of vice, adding sin to sin every day and hour of your life. This is just because when you mortally sin you lose all right to any help from God.

Sadly, you act freely when you sin, for no one forces you to do wrong. However, when you fall you can't rise without divine assistance that He doesn't owe you. He gives this gratuitous gift when He restores you to His favor. Conversely, He exercises His justice when He permits you to remain in misery, and even to fall lower.

Tremble for your salvation while always maintaining an unshaken hope, but have no less fear of Hell. You've no reason to expect that God will treat you differently from anyone else. Bear in mind the law of His justice and never expose yourself to its terrible effects here or hereafter.

Chapter 27

Of Those who Allege that the Path of Virtue is too Difficult

Virtue has nothing in its own nature that makes it burdensome. The difficulty with living a virtuous life comes from evil inclinations and appetites for sin. When Adam and Eve rebelled against God, their passions rebelled against reason and from this arose all the difficulties of living a virtuous life. Thus, many appreciate virtue but refuse to practice it, just as sick people desire health, but refuse the unpalatable remedies that might restore it.

The principal cause of this problem comes from focusing only on the obstacles to virtue and not the graces God provides to overcome them. Don't forget that God wants to pardon you and help you avoid future sins. Remember that Jesus came to help you work on your salvation. He died to destroy sin and instituted the sacraments to strengthen you against sin.

Remember that virtues flow from His grace to sweeten the yoke of Christ, to facilitate the practice of virtue, to make you joyful in tribulations, hopeful in danger, and victorious in temptation. This comprises the teaching of the Gospel. Adam, an earthly and sinful man, made us earthly and sinful. Jesus

Christ, a heavenly and just Man, makes us spiritual and just. Jesus assures that in addition to all this, He'll give you the necessary strength to overcome the passions that torment you. With such assistance, you can overcome temptations and not fear your evil inclinations.

Some argue that they've so many sins that God will refuse His grace. Perish the thought, you're insulting God! By it, you say either that God can't or won't help you. Don't yield to such a blasphemy. Rather pray, as St. Augustine taught. "Give me grace, Lord, to do what you command and command what you please." (Conf. L.10, 31) God always answers this prayer for He always cooperates when you seek to do His will. He'll help like a master painter guiding the hand of a pupil.

Let these words assure you that however difficult God's commandments may appear, His grace will make observing them very easy. And if you remain faithful to them, you'll soon know His yoke as sweetness and His burden light.

Moreover, remember how charity helps you pursue virtue. Charity, or the love of God, makes the law sweet and delightful, for as St. Augustine said, "Love knows no fatigue." How willingly people fond of hunting, riding, or fishing bear the labor of these sports. Love makes a mother insensible to the fatigue she endures for her child. Love keeps a devoted wife day and night at the bedside of her sick husband. Filled with this power, St. Paul exclaimed, "What will separate us from the love of Christ? Will anguish, or distress, or persecution, or famine, or nakedness, or peril, or the sword?" (Rom. 8:35)

Though trials and difficulties always come your way, the path of the wicked has many more hardships than that of the just. One necessarily grows weary on a long journey, but a blind man who stumbles at every step certainly tires sooner than the traveler who can see clearly. The sinner, guided by passion, walks blindly and therefore often falls. The just, guided by reason, sees and avoids the rocks and precipices, and travels with less fatigue and more safely.

Nothing provides greater astonishment or a more interesting spectacle than the action of the Holy Spirit upon a just person. How it transforms, sustains, strengthens, and comforts them. How it alters their affections, makes them love what they formerly abhorred, and abhor what they formerly loved. What peace it gives them. What light it pours into their souls to enable them to learn God's will, to realize the vanity of the world, and to set a true value on the spiritual blessings that they formerly despised. Still more wonderful is how quickly they make these changes. They don't spend years studying, or wait until old age helps them by experience. People in the fire of youth sometimes change in the space of a few days and hardly seem the same beings. Hence, St. Cyprian says that the sinner finds himself converted without knowing how to make such a change, for grace does the work. The change needs neither study nor time and acts in an instant like a spiritual charm.

Behold the power of grace! What, then, prevents you from following this path? If you believe what I have related and that God wants to give you this grace, what prevents you from breaking your sinful bonds and embracing Jesus who so lovingly is calling you? Why do you prefer this hell on earth, to gain another hell hereafter, rather than by a paradise here, gain Heaven hereafter? Don't despair, put your trust in God and resolutely enter the path of virtue. Have an unshaken confidence that you'll meet Him there with open arms, to receive you as the father received his prodigal son.

Someday you'll acknowledge these truths, if not in this life, then in the next. Think of the confusion and anguish on the day of your judgment when God condemns you for not following the path of virtue. Too late, you'll recognize the excellence of this path that leads to eternal joy.

Chapter 28

Of those who Refuse to Practice Virtue because They Love the World

In the hearts of those who refuse to practice virtue, we frequently find delusive love for the world as the chief cause of their faintheartedness. I call it a delusive love because it relies on the imaginary good they think they can find in the things of this world. If they examine more closely the objects of their affection, they'd soon recognize that they pursue shadows. If we study the happiness of the world, even under its most favorable aspects, drawbacks always lessen its sweetness.

The first is brevity. We all know the shortness of human life. Very few attain even a hundred years. Popes have reigned but a month. Bishops have survived their consecration but little longer, and some brides' funerals follow within days of their weddings. These things happened in the past and in every age. Suppose, however, that your life will be one of the longest. St. John Chrysostom asked, "What are one hundred, two hundred, four hundred years spent in the pleasures of this world compared to eternity?"

All happiness, however great, remains but a brief vanity when compared to eternity. What has become of the scholars and the searchers into the secrets of nature? Where is the famous Alexander? Where are the Caesars and the other kings of the earth? It gains them nothing now that they lived in pomp and glory, that they had legions of soldiers and servants and flatterers almost without number. All have vanished like a shadow or a dream. In one moment, all that constitutes human happiness fades away like mist before the morning sun. Behold, then, dear Christian, the brevity of your life.

Consider also the innumerable changes that attack your happiness in this valley of tears. Your days scarcely suffice to number your sorrows, for almost every hour brings new cares, new anxieties, or new miseries. You can't count all the infirmities of the body, all the passions of the soul, all the disasters that come upon you from enemies, and even from friends and yourself. One disputes your inheritance and another tries to kill you. Hatred, envy, and revenge pursue you. Finally, add to these the miseries and the innumerable accidents which daily befall you.

To understand the world better, consider who governs it. Jesus teaches that the devil is the prince of this world. Judge, by the picture I have painted, how much reason you've to hate a world so full of corruption and where evil spirits and crimes outnumber the rays of the sun. Nourish and increase the desire to fly, at least in spirit, from this world, saying with David, "If only I had wings like a dove that I might fly away and find rest." (Ps. 54:7)

I must emphasize one of the world's most evil characteristics, its delusive appearance. This world pretends to be what it isn't, promises what it can't give, and allures us to eternal ruin. Just like a jewel can be real or fake, there is real and counterfeit happiness. Aristotle says that a falsehood sometimes has more appearance of truth than truth, so many evil things appear better than truly good things. The happiness of the world falls into this category and allures the ignorant as glittering bait draws fish to their death. Worldly things present themselves with bright and smiling exteriors that promise great joy. However, experience soon dissipates your illusions and you feel the sting of the hook almost as soon as you take the bait.

How attractive honors, dignities, and awards appear. However, what anxieties, what jealousies, what passions, and what hardships their false splendors conceal. Consider, for example, unlawful love. Such entanglements present a pleasing prospect to the senses, but once sinners enter this dark labyrinth, they quickly become the victim of a thousand harrowing torments. A furious dragon guards this forbidden tree. With the sword of an injured parent or a jealous husband, he frequently deprives the sinner of reputation, honor, fortune, life, and soul.

The song of human glory lures us to destruction, attracting us only to deceive, and elevating only to crush. Consider the return it exacts for all that it gives. Grief at the loss of a child far exceeds the joy of its birth. Loss supplies more pain than profit provides joy. The affliction of sickness far exceeds the pleasure of health. Insults wound more than honors flatter. Life dispenses joys and sorrows so unequally that the latter have greater impact than the former. These reflections manifestly prove the delusiveness of worldly happiness.

Behold what a striking representation of Hell the world provides. Hell is a place of sin and suffering and in the world, these evils also abound. Everywhere we find sin and punishment. Hence, St. Bernard said that without the hope of a better life, little difference would exist between this world and hell. (Serm. 4 de Ascen.)

You only find true happiness in God. No creature can enjoy perfect happiness until it has attained its highest degree of perfection. Until it has reached this, it can't rest, nor can it find perfect happiness because it still needs something to satisfy itself. As a glove is made for the hand, and the scabbard for the sword, so is the human heart created for God. In Him alone, you can know happiness. Your ultimate attainment of happiness, or your highest degree of perfection, depends on God. He is your beginning and your end.

You need nothing else to follow these wise examples and embrace so great a good. No greater obligation exists than the one that binds you to serve God. You've seen that all other obligations pale in comparison. If benefits move you, no benefit compares with creation and redemption. Nothing provides eternal joy better than avoiding eternal misery. The least joy of virtue provides more happiness than the possession of all the treasures of the world. If you reject these ideas, you do so in willful blindness, for you close your eyes to the light of truth.

Chapter 29

The First Remedy Against Sin:
A Firm Resolution not to Commit it

I must do more than persuade you to love virtue, I must teach you how to acquire it. First, you can't have vices. Therefore, I'll begin with the most common vices and their remedies.

To change your life and give yourself to God, make this task your sole interest and hold it in your heart as the sole wisdom of the world by pursuing it vigorously and with determination. Recognize the dangers you encounter fade to nothingness compared to your goal. Understand that soon after you set out on this journey, Hell will send out its forces against you. The flesh, corrupted from birth, will assail you with insatiable desires and alluring pleasures. Evil habits as strong as nature itself will fiercely resist and exaggerate the difficulties you face.

To turn a river from its course takes less effort than to change a life mired in bad habits. The world, powerful and cruel, will wage a fierce war against you. Armed with its pleasures and bad examples, it will hasten to ensure your downfall. It will try to captivate your heart with pomp and vanities and boldly attack you with ridicule and persecution. The devil himself, the arch-deceiver, will renew his warfare and turn all his forces against you. Enraged at your desertion from his party, he will leave nothing undone to ruin you.

Prepare yourself for these difficulties and stay focused on the glorious prize. Remember, your nearby powerful defenders remain ready to defend you against the snares of the devil. Against the allurements of evil habits, you have the force of good habits confirmed by God's grace. Against the bad example and persecutions of the world, you have the good example and strengthening exhortations of the saints. Against the sinful pleasures and vain joys of the world, you have the pure joys and ineffable consolations of the Holy Spirit.

Resting on these principles, make a deep and unshaken resolution never to commit mortal sin, for it will rob you of God's grace and friendship. Such a resolution insures a virtuous life. As long as you persevere, you possess the divine charity that makes you a child of God and gives you access to the blessings of the Church and the Kingdom of Heaven. Finally, avoid venial sin because it weakens you and disposes you to mortal sin.

Chapter 30

Remedies against Pride

SECTION I
General Remedies

The deadly or capital sins provide the source for all iniquities. They form the roots of the mighty tree of vice, and if you can destroy them, the trunk and branches soon decay. St. Thomas taught that all sin proceeds from self-love, for you never commit sin without coveting some gratification for self. Three of the deadly sins, lust, gluttony, and sloth, spring from love of pleasure, pride springs from love of honors, and covetousness from love of riches. The remaining two, anger and envy, serve all these unlawful loves. Anger rouses when any obstacle prevents you from attaining your desires, and envy grows when you see someone possessing what you claim. These provide the roots of the seven deadly sins, so vigorously attack these mighty giants.

First, attack the most formidable of these enemies: pride. Pride provides that inordinate desire of your own excellence, which spiritual writers universally regard as the father of all the other vices. Whenever this vice attacks, reflect on the terrible punishment the angels brought upon themselves by the sin of pride. God cast them from Heaven into the lowest depths of Hell. Consider how this fall transformed Lucifer, the prince of the angelic hosts. In one moment, he lost all his glory and became not only a demon but the chief of all demons. If pure spirits received such punishment, know that you'll receive no less, as God never changes or makes exceptions for anyone before His justice.

God hates pride while humility pleases Him. St. Augustine said, "Humility makes men angels, and pride makes angels devils." Reflect on Christ's astonishing example of humility. Because of His love of us, He took on a nature infinitely beneath His own, and "became obedient unto death, death on the cross." (Phil. 2:8) Learn from His example and humble yourself. Appreciate your baseness. Learn to be "meek and humble of heart." (Matt. 11:29)

Consider your birth, life and death. Before your birth you grew from an unformed mass. Now corruption fills you, and in a little while, worms will feed upon you. If you take pride in your riches and worldly position, remember that in a few years death makes everyone equal with one important exception, those who possessed most during life will have the most to account for.

St. Chrysostom said to examine the graves of the rich and powerful and try to find some trace of the luxury in which they lived, or the pleasures they so eagerly enjoyed. Nothing remains of their magnificent retinues and costly adornments. You won't find any of their ingenious devices destined to gratify their senses and banish their weariness. Nothing remains of their sumptuous banquets. You won't hear their laughter but only the somber silence that reigns in these homes of the dead. Look at the bodies that they loved too much and you see nothing but dust and ashes, worms and corruption.

This fate awaits no matter how well you take care of yourself. If only the evil ended here, but worse can follow death. I speak here of the dread tribunal of God's justice, the sentence passed upon the guilty, the weeping and gnashing of teeth, the tortures of the worm that never dies, and the fire which never goes out.

Also, consider the danger of bragging, the daughter of pride, which St. Bernard said "enters lightly but wounds deeply." Therefore, when people praise you, think whether you really possess the qualities for which they commend you. Don't rely upon the vain commendations of others, but upon what you really know of yourself. Though others extol you to the skies, listen to the warnings of your conscience and accept the testimony of this intimate friend rather than those praising you. Commit your glory to the care of God, whose wisdom will preserve it for you and whose fidelity will restore it to you in the sight of angels and people.

SECTION II
Particular Remedies

Since humility comes from knowledge of self, pride springs from ignorance of self. To find humility, look into your heart with the light of truth and see the stains of sinful pleasures, thousands of mistakes, and fears. Study yourself with serious attention and you'll find nothing to be proud of.

Don't swell with pride when you compare yourself with those you consider less virtuous. If you yield to this temptation, remember that though you may surpass your neighbor in some virtues, in others you likely fall way behind. Focus on what you lack, and not on what you possess.

Study your neighbor's virtues rather than your own. This will keep you humble and increase your desire for perfection.

However, if you focus on your virtues and look at other people's failings you'll naturally prefer yourself. This satisfaction with yourself will prevent you from making further advances.

If you find yourself inclined to take pride in a good action, carefully watch the feelings of your heart, bearing in mind that this satisfaction will destroy the merits of your labor. Attribute no good to yourself, but refer everything to God. Repress all suggestions of pride with the beautiful words of the great Apostle, "What do you possess that you have not received? But if you have received it, why are you boasting as if you did not receive it?" (1Cor. 4:7)

When you feel pride rising in your heart, apply a remedy immediately. For example, recall all your sins, particularly the most shameful. Like a wise doctor, you'll counteract the effect of one poison with another.

Finally, patiently bear persecution, for it provides a clear path to humility. Never despise the poor and abject, for their misery should move you to compassion rather than contempt. Don't yearn for rich apparel, for love of display negates humility. Too much concern about your appearance makes you a slave to the opinions of others. However, don't go to extremes and dress in a manner unsuited to your position. While claiming to despise the approbation or notice of the world, many secretly strive for it by their exaggerated simplicity. Finally, don't disdain humble and obscure employments. Only the proud avoid these, for a person of true humility deems nothing beneath him.

Chapter 31

Remedies Against Covetousness

SECTION I
Against Covetousness in General

Covetousness is an inordinate desire for riches. We see this in people who not only steal, but who also passionately long for others' goods or too eagerly cling to their own. With great force, St. Paul condemned this vice and declared it the source of all iniquity. He said, "Those who want to be rich are falling into temptation and into a trap and into many foolish and harmful desires, which plunge them into ruin and destruction. For the love of money is the root of all evils, and some people in their desire for it have strayed from the faith and have pierced themselves with many pains." (1 Tim. 6:9-10)

When this vice assails you, remember that Jesus disdained riches and desired no objects. On the contrary, He so loved poverty that He chose for His Mother not a rich and powerful queen, but a poor and humble Virgin. He willed His birth not in a palace, but in a bleak stable, and chose a straw-filled manger for His bed. During His time on earth, He always showed His love for poverty and His contempt for riches. Finally, He chose poor and ignorant fishermen for his apostles, not the princes of great houses.

Consider that Jesus didn't give His life for this material world, but He gave it for your soul that He considered far more valuable. You can't find true riches in silver, or gold, or precious stones, but in virtue, the inseparable companion of a good conscience. Set aside the vain opinions of society and you'll understand that these metals only get their value from the opinion of the world. St. Jerome said that someone who guards their riches like a slave becomes their victim, but someone who throws off their yoke possesses them as their lord and master.

Consider yet another truth. The more worldly prosperity you enjoy, the less likely you'll have spiritual riches because having an abundance of things leads to trusting them rather than God. Ironically, prosperity increases your misery. The desire for and the love of riches provides greater torment than the pleasure you gain from owning them. They entangle you in thousands of temptations and under the delusive image of pleasure, plunge you into an inexhaustible source of trouble, disquiet, and sin. Worse than all this, you rarely accumulate them without offending God, for a rich man is either a wicked man or a wicked man's heir.

Moreover, if you possessed all the riches in the world, they wouldn't satisfy the desires of your heart. However many possessions you accumulate, they never fill the void within you. Your insatiable thirst for possessions destroys the enjoyment of the possessions you already have.

Free yourself from the worry of acquiring possessions, put yourself in the hands of God, and fully confide in His providence. He never forsakes those who trust in Him. Since He requires you to seek food, He won't permit you to perish from hunger. God, who cares for the birds of the air and clothes the lilies of the field, won't show indifference to the necessities of one of His noblest creatures. Life passes quickly and every moment brings death nearer, so don't store up provisions that will only impede your progress for such a short journey.

When you reach the end of a life poor in this world's goods, your wealth of real treasure far exceeds that of the greedy, who spend their lives accumulating riches. How differently God will judge you, and how willingly you'll part with your few possessions you value so little. But the rich and the covetous, in addition to the terrible judgment they face, will fill with anguish at parting from the wealth they love and adore.

You'll suffer great misfortune if death finds you unprepared. Fate waits to divide your body as food for worms, your soul as the victim of demons, and your wealth as the prey of eager, ungrateful, and extravagant heirs. Better to follow the counsel of Jesus and share your wealth with the poor, so angels will bear it before you into Heaven.

I remind you that God, as a wise and sovereign ruler, has appointed some of His children the depositaries of His power and the dispensers of His benefits. Contribute your surplus possessions to the poor and don't take for yourself what God has given you for the benefit of others. St. Basil said, "The bread you withhold is the food of the poor, the garments you conceal should clothe the naked, and the gold you accumulate belongs to the needy."

Therefore, you rob the poor when you refuse to help them. Use the riches you receive from God to remedy human misery, not as instruments of a bad life. Don't let your prosperity cause you to forget the Author of all your blessings, or to fill you with pride. Find contentment in the condition God has placed you, bearing in mind the words of the Apostle, "If we have food and clothing, we shall be content with that." (1 Tim. 6:8)

Remember that virtue doesn't lie in poverty but in the love of poverty. Hence, all who voluntarily forsake wealth bear a striking resemblance to Our Savior, who, filled with the riches of God, lived poor for love of us. Those compelled to live in poverty and bear it with patience, never coveting the wealth, convert their necessity into a meritorious virtue. As the poor by their poverty conform themselves to Jesus Christ, so the rich by their alms conform their hearts to the merciful Heart of Jesus.

If God bestows you with wealth, give it generously to the poor, assured that it accumulates as treasure for you in the kingdom of Heaven. However, if you waste the means God gives you, don't expect to find any treasure when you leave this life. Store up, by a worthy use of your worldly wealth, a store of spiritual possessions that not even death can take away.

SECTION II
Against the unjust Detention of Another's Goods

Theft consists in unjustly taking what belongs to another, and unlawfully retaining it against the owner's will. Your intention to restore it later doesn't suffice if you can do it at once, for restitution demands promptness. Inability to make immediate restitution justifies deferring it while in poverty. Inability to ever make restitution excuses you entirely, for God doesn't require the impossible.

If you perform the duties of executor of a will, don't defraud the departed soul of the help you owe. Pay your dependants regularly, and keep your accounts carefully, so they don't cause disputes after your death. Don't expect your survivors to carry out your last wishes, but fulfill them yourself as far as you can. For if you handle your affairs carelessly, know that others won't do any better.

Make it a point of honor to owe no one, and you'll enjoy peaceful slumber, a quiet conscience, a contented life, and a happy death. Control your desires and appetites and govern your expenditures by your income, not by your caprices. Your debts proceed from ill-regulated, uncontrolled desires more than from necessities, and consequently moderation provides more profit than the largest revenues.

Understand that the only real riches, the only real treasures, come from abandoning covetousness and pursuing justice, Godliness, faith, charity, patience, and mildness. Find contentment with the position God has placed you in, for you can never know happiness by striving against the will of God.

Chapter 32

Remedies against Lust

SECTION I
General Remedies

Lust is an inordinate desire for unlawful or immoral pleasures. This most widespread vice attacks most violently and remains the most insatiable. St. Augustine said that Christians must defend their chastity through the severest of combat, for battles rage frequently and we seldom achieve victories.

Whenever this shameful vice attacks, resist it as follows: First, remember that this disorder both stains your soul and defiles your body in which the Holy Body of Christ lives. Secondly, consider that this deplorable vice necessarily causes the spiritual ruin of those who participate in your crime.

This treacherous vice begins in pleasure, but ends in an abyss of bitterness and remorse. Nothing more easily draws a person and nothing keeps you tighter in its grasp. The flattering aspects attract, then when you accept the sinful yoke and cast aside all shame, it requires almost a miracle of grace to free yourself from this degrading bondage. It's like a fisherman's net, which the fish easily enter but from which they rarely escape. In addition, many other sins spring from this vice, for while in its grasp, you often offend God by thoughts, words, desires, and actions.

Lust robs your reputation and rapidly undermines your strength, exhausts your energy, and withers your beauty via foul and loathsome diseases. It robs youth of its freshness and hurries you toward premature and dishonorable old age. It penetrates your soul, darkens understanding, obscures memories, and weakens your will. It turns you from every noble and honorable work, burying you so deeply in the mire of impurity, you only think and speak of vileness.

This vice also promotes gluttony, drinking, and drugs. Victims squander their wealth on rich apparel, sumptuous living, costly jewels, and rich adornments. The example of the prodigal son, exhausting his inheritance in these pleasures, shows the evil of this passion.

The more you indulge in these infamous gratifications, the more your desire grows insatiable. If you compare the fleeting nature of these pleasures with the enduring punishment they bring, you'll realize the stupidity of your choice. St. Gregory taught that pleasure lasts but a moment, but suffering endures eternally. (Moral. 9, 44)

If you've fallen victim to this sin, restore the beauty of the Creator's work by giving yourself to His service with a zeal and fervor born of deep gratitude for forgiven sin, and with an ardent desire to repair the past. St. Gregory said that often people with tepid and indifferent faith become strong and fervent soldiers of Christ through repentance. (Past. p1) Finally, since God continued to preserve your life after you so basely offended Him, profit by this opportunity to serve Him and make reparation for your sins before another fall crushes you.

SECTION II
Particular Remedies

Besides these general remedies, I have some others. First, vigorously resist the first attacks of vice. If you don't resist the initial attack, it rapidly acquires strength and enters your soul. Secondly, carefully guard your senses, particularly the eyes, and don't look at anything capable of exciting sinful desires. Third, protect your ears from impure conversation. If someone utters harsh words in your presence, indicate your displeasure by at least a grave and serious look, for what you hear with pleasure you learn to do with complacency. Guard your tongue carefully and don't use immodest words because "evil communications," says the Apostle, "corrupt good morals." (1Cor. 15:33) Occupy your mind and body with good thoughts and deeds "...because the devil," says St. Bernard, "fills idle souls with bad thoughts, so that they may think of evil even if they don't actually commit it."

In all temptations, but particularly in temptations against purity, remember the presence of your guardian angel and of the devil, your accuser, for they both witness all your actions and will render an account of them to Him who sees and judges all things. Remember the terrible tribunal of God's judgment and the eternal flames of Hell.

In addition, guard your conversations with the opposite sex. Don't spend time alone with them. St. Chrysostom warned that the enemy attacks men and women more vigorously when he finds them alone. His boldness grows when no witnesses can thwart his plans. Avoid the society of people not above suspicion, for their words inflame the heart, their glances wound the soul, and everything about them traps those who visit them with imprudent familiarity. Don't participate in the improper interchange of presents, visits, or letters, for these will entangle you and awaken dangerous affections. In all friendships with virtuous people, respect them deeply and avoid seeing them too often or conversing too familiarly with them.

Chapter 33

Remedies against Envy

Envy consists of feeling bad about the good fortune or happiness of others. Envy leads to mortal sin because it directly opposes charity. Envy, a very powerful sin, has spread all over the world but we find it most often among the rich and powerful.

History abounds with examples of this fatal vice that caused the first fratricide when Cain killed Abel. Envy existed between the brothers Romulus and Remus, the founders of Rome. We see it in Joseph's brothers who sold him into slavery (Gen. 37) and between Aaron and Mary, the brother and sister of Moses. (Num. 12) Even the disciples of Our Lord had it before the coming of the Holy Ghost.

Diligently arm yourself against envy and unceasingly ask God to deliver you from it. If it attacks, oppose it with strong resistance, and make little account of the unworthy sentiments it suggests. If your neighbor enjoys prosperity, thank God for it. Know that envying the prosperity of others doesn't alleviate your misery, but only increases it.

To strengthen your aversion to this vice, consider how closely envious people resemble devils, who look with rage upon your good works and the heavenly rewards you'll receive for them. With no hope of such heavenly happiness, they try to steal from you. For this reason, St. Augustine prayed that God preserve everyone from this vice of devils that causes hopeless suffering.

Consider how envy corrodes the heart, weakens the understanding, destroys all peace of soul, and condemns one to a melancholy and intolerable existence. Its ravages extend even to the countenance, whose paleness testifies to the passion that rages within. Envy subjects you to severe tortures. Hence, some call it a just vice, because it inflicts its own punishment.

Consider how envy opposes charity. When you envy another's good, when you hate those in whom God manifests His love, you strive to undo God's work.

Fight envy by loving humility and hating pride, the father of envy. Proud people who can't stand superiors or equals persuade themselves that they descend in proportion as others rise.

Wean your heart from worldly honors and possessions and seek only spiritual riches, for such treasures don't diminish when enjoyed in quantity, but actually increase.

Don't settle for feeling good at your neighbor's prosperity, but try to help them all you can, and the good you can't give them ask God to grant them. Hate no one. Love your friends and your enemies for God.

Your neighbor may be wicked, but don't hate him. In such a case, imitate the example of a wise physician, who loves his patients but hates their diseases. Abhor sin but love your neighbor. Remember the benefits God unceasingly gives you. Know that all He asks in return is that you be charitable and generous, not to Him, for He has no need of you or your possessions, but to your neighbor, whom He has recommended to your love.

Chapter 34

Remedies against Gluttony

Gluttony is the inordinate love of eating and drinking. Our Savior warned against this vice, saying, "Beware that your hearts do not become drowsy from carousing and drunkenness and the anxieties of daily life..." (Lk 21: 34)

When you feel the promptings of this shameful disorder remember gluttony brought death into the world. The devil first tempted Jesus with gluttony, wishing to open a path for all other vices to find an easy entrance.

Consider Our Lord's extraordinary fast in the desert and the rigorous mortifications He imposed upon His Sacred Body. He did this to expiate your excesses and to provide a good example. You can't call yourself a follower of Christ if when He fasts, you abandon yourself to food and drink.

If you find abstinence difficult, remember the gall and vinegar the soldiers gave Jesus on the cross. Reflect on the terrible austerities and wonderful fasts observed by the desert Fathers and how they fled from the world to remote solitude. Here, after the example of Christ, they crucified their flesh with all its irregular appetites and sustained by God's grace, subsisted for many years on roots and herbs.

You can't gain Heaven by a path of gross and sensual pleasures. Think of the innumerable poor who need bread.

Then blush to make the gifts of God's bounty instruments of gluttony. Consider how often the Sacred Host rests upon your tongue, and don't permit sin to enter through the gate through which God nourishes your soul.

Govern your appetite by reason and don't let the snares of this vice, disguised as necessities, deceive you. Your soul can only rule the flesh when it submits to God. Let God command your reason and reason will properly direct your soul.

If tempted by gluttony, remember that you've already tasted its pleasures and they didn't last very long. They passed like a dream, the way light of day dispels the night. However, the remorse for gluttony remains long after its pleasures depart. When you overcome this enemy, you'll experience consolation and peace.

I offer a final thought for your consideration. If you perform a virtuous act with difficulty, the difficulty soon passes and the joy of virtue remains, but if you take pleasure in committing a base act, the pleasure disappears quickly, but its shame stays with you. (Aul. Gel., Noct. Attic. 8, 15)

Chapter 35

Remedies against Anger and Hatred

Anger is an inordinate desire for revenge. St. Paul spoke strongly against it saying, "Put away all bitterness, anger, indignation, clamor, and blasphemy. Be kind, merciful, and forgiving to each other as God forgives you in Christ." (Eph. 4:31-32) Our Savior Himself said, "But I say to you, whoever is angry with his brother will be liable to judgment…" (Matt. 5:22) You disgrace yourself when you indulge in ungovernable rage like a wild animal.

If you find it hard to subdue anger caused by your neighbor, consider how much more God has borne from you and how He has endured you. Your sins helped crucify Him when He shed the last drop of His Blood, yet He bears with sweet patience your daily offenses against Him.

If anger makes you believe your enemy doesn't deserve forgiveness, ask yourself if you deserve God's pardon. Don't expect God to grant you mercy when you hate your neighbor. If your neighbor doesn't deserve pardon from you, you don't deserve pardon from God. Remember, you only merit God's pardon because of Jesus' sacrifice for you. Therefore, for love of Him, forgive all who offend you.

Know that as long as hatred fills your heart, you can't offer anything acceptable to God. Jesus taught this when He said, "Therefore, if you bring your gift to the altar, and there recall that your brother has anything against you, leave your gift there at the altar, go first and be reconciled with your brother, and then come and offer your gift." (Matt. 5:23-24) Hence, the sin of enmity between you and your neighbor creates enmity between you and God and destroys the merit of all your good works. St. Gregory says, "You gain no merit from good works if you don't endure injuries with patience." (Moral. 21:16)

Your neighbor is either a just person or a sinner. What a great misfortune to offend God by treating a just neighbor badly. What a shame to plunge your soul into sin if they're a sinner. Finally, if your neighbor seeks vengeance for the injury you inflict, your problems will never end.

St. Paul taught about noble revenge when he said not to let evil overcome you, rather overcome it with good. (Rom. 12:21) When you seek revenge, anger often defeats and ultimately disappoints you. However, when you overcome your passion, you gain a glorious victory. Ultimately, you win the noblest triumphs by controlling your passion with reason.

Anger makes you say and do inappropriate things. This makes it imperative that you oppose, with all your strength, the suggestions of passion. If you can't, you'll be like an intoxicated person who acts unreasonably and afterwards feels remorse. Anger, wine, and sensuality make for evil counselors. Keep in mind that God holds you responsible for sins committed in such a state.

Thus, make a firm resolution never to speak or act under the influence of anger, nor to heed any suggestions, however plausible, which your heart may urge at such moments. Never act until your anger subsides or until you once or twice repeat the Our Father or some other prayer.

Thinking of other things also provides a good remedy. Try to banish from your mind the subject that irritates you because when you take away the fuel of a fire, the flame soon expires. Try to love the one who troubles you, for patience unaccompanied with love often changes into hatred. Hence, St. Paul taught that charity is patient and kind (1Cor. 13:4) for true charity loves those whom it patiently endures. Finally, if you anger your neighbor, quietly withdraw until their passion subsides, or at least answer them with mildness, for, "A mild answer calms wrath, but a harsh word stirs up anger." (Prov. 15:1)

Chapter 36

Remedies against Sloth

Sloth is a reluctance to do what is expected of you and having distaste for spiritual things. Jesus clearly exhorted His disciples to diligence, the opposite of sloth, when He told them to watch and pray, for they didn't know when the Lord of the house would come. (Mk. 13:35) Banish this shameful vice by doing the following things.

Remember the extraordinary labors Our Lord endured for you. Recall the many sleepless nights He spent in prayer for you, His weary journeys from city to city healing the sick, comforting the sorrowful, and raising the dead. How ardently and unceasingly He worked for your redemption. Consider how, for the love of you, He carried on His bruised and bleeding shoulders that heavy cross. If the God of majesty labored so hard to deliver you, don't refuse to cooperate in your own salvation. Remember also the weary labors of the Apostles, who preached the Gospel everywhere they went. Think of the sufferings endured by the martyrs, confessors, virgins, hermits, and by all who now reign with Christ. Through their teaching and work, the Faith of Christ spread through the world and the Church perpetuates it to the present day.

Turn your eyes toward nature and you find nothing idle. The heavens, by their perpetual motion, unceasingly proclaim the glory of their Creator. The sun, moon, and stars, with all the brilliant planets, constantly follow their courses. Plants and trees continually grow. Watch the untiring energy of ants who labor for their winter food or how bees build their hives and fill them with honey. These industrious little creatures don't allow an idler to exist among them. Profit by your work now, because a day will come when you won't have these opportunities. Sad experience teaches that many fall prey to this disappointment. Life is short, and obstacles to do good abound. Don't let the promptings of sloth let you miss an opportunity that will never return, for "...Night is coming when no one can work." (Jn. 9:4)

The number and enormity of your sins demands a proportionate fervor for penance. St. Peter denied Jesus three times, but never ceased to weep for his sin though Jesus pardoned him. St. Mary Magdalene always bewailed the disorders of her youth, though Jesus said to her, "Your sins are forgiven." Many people who have returned to God continue to do penance for their sins throughout their lives, though many of them offended God far less grievously than you.

Every day you pile up sins, so don't consider any labor too severe to expiate them. Profit by your remaining time of grace and mercy to do works of penance to purchase eternal peace. Your paltry and insignificant works unite with the merits of Christ and acquire infinite value. The labor takes a short time but your reward continues for eternity.

Chapter 37

Other Sins to Avoid

SECTION I
On Taking the Name of God in Vain

Besides the seven capital sins, a good Christian avoids these other sins with equal diligence. Don't take God's name in vain. This sin directly attacks God's majesty and offends Him more than any sin against your neighbor. You commit mortal sin when you swear by God's Holy name, and when you swear by the cross, by the saints, or by your own salvation if taken falsely.

Don't settle for merely avoiding the vice of taking God's name in vain. Cringe in horror when others commit it, and reprove it whenever you encounter it. If you inadvertently fall into it, impose some penance of prayer or alms to punish yourself, and to impress on your mind the determination to avoid it in the future.

All of this applies equally to blasphemy and perjury. Also, beware of cursing. Use God's name only with devotion and affection. Strive to speak with piety the holy name of God and by your prayers, exhortations, and example banish the terrible evil of taking the Lord's name in vain.

SECTION II
On Detraction

The abominable sin of detraction pervades society. Those infected with this sin can't bear to hear anything good about another person. Instead, they focus on their neighbor's faults and at every opportunity tear their character to pieces.

To turn you away from this detestable and dangerous vice, consider that it always borders upon mortal sin. You commit detraction when you tell about another's real faults. When you criticize their minor failings, the sin is venial, but if you mention some hidden and grave fault the sin is mortal.

The sin harms the one who speaks, those who listen with approval, and the victim. In addition, the person who complacently listens to the detraction frequently spreads the tale to others. Worse yet, to ingratiate themselves to the victim, they often tell the victim what they heard. This can excite long-lasting hatreds and even bloodshed.

The sin also ruins your reputation. People fly from a detractor as naturally as they do from a venomous snake. Abhor this terrible vice and don't make yourself odious in the sight of God and people for a sin that brings you no advantage. Remember that this vice quickly becomes habit and every time you speak with others, you expose yourself to the danger of relapsing.

Consider your neighbor's character a forbidden tree that you can't touch. Be equally slow in praising yourself as in censuring others, for the first indicates vanity and the second a want of charity. Speak of the virtues of your neighbors but remain silent about their faults. Always help others think your neighbors glow with virtue and honor and you'll avoid innumerable sins and much remorse of conscience. You'll please God and others will respect you.

Don't detract from others, and avoid hearing this sin and show detractors how displeasing you find their conduct. If possible, respond with silence, try to turn the conversation, or show that you find the conversation displeasing. Beware of hearing the detractor with smiling attention, for you'll encourage them and consequently share in their guilt. You commit a grievous offense if you set fire to a house, and remain scarcely less culpable if you stand idly by witnessing its destruction instead of helping to put it out.

Of all detractions, the worst occurs when directed against a virtuous person, for it injures the person assailed, discourages others striving for virtue, and confirms the cowardice of those not willing to try. To appreciate the evil of this kind of scandal, reflect upon what Jesus said, "Whoever causes one of these little ones who believe in me to sin, it would be better for him to have a great millstone hung around his neck and to be drowned in the depths of the sea." (Matt. 18:6) Avoid, therefore, as you would a sacrilege, all scandalous reflections upon persons consecrated to God. Even if their conduct provides matters for censure, continue to respect their sacred character.

SECTION III
On Rash Judgments

If you commit the sin of detraction, you usually don't confine yourself to what you know, but indulge in suppositions and rash judgments. You'll likely invent evil intentions, misinterpret good actions, and forget that Our Savior said, "Don't judge that you may not be judged. For as you judge, so will you be judged, and the measure with which you measure will be measured out to you." (Matt. 7:1-2)

SECTION IV
On the Commandments of the Church

Besides these sins against the Commandments of God, follow the commandments of the Church, which also impose grave obligations. Such as to attend Mass on Sundays and Holy Days of Obligation, to confess your sins at least once a year, to receive the Holy Eucharist at Easter, to support the Church insofar as you are able, and to observe the days of fasting and abstinence prescribed by the Church. The precept of fasting binds from the age of 21, and abstinence obliges all who have attained the age of reason. Those exempt from fasting include the sick, the convalescent, nursing women, women in pregnancy, those whose labors are severe, and those who are too poor to afford one full meal a day. Other lawful reasons exist for dispensation, for which you'll need the permission of your pastor. Don't take it upon yourself to set aside the law of the Church.

Chapter 38

Venial Sins

Avoid venial sins. Some ungenerous Christians have no problem committing venial sins. St. Augustine said to fear venial sins because they accumulate like drops of water and form a raging river that sweeps everything away.

Venial sins weaken your devotion, trouble your conscience, diminish charity, exhaust your spiritual life, and obstruct the work of the Holy Spirit. I pray you do all in your power to avoid them, for even weak enemies can harm you if you don't resist. I warn you to avoid slight anger, gluttony, vanity, idle words and thoughts, immoderate laughter, loss of time, too much sleeping, and trivial lies or flatteries. Have great vigilance against these kinds of offenses for opportunities for venial sin abound.

Chapter 39

Shorter Remedies against Sins, particularly the Seven Deadly Sins

The following short considerations will help you during the moment of temptation.

In temptations to pride, reflect upon the depth of humility Jesus descended to for love of you and know however profound a contempt others have for you, you deserve to be more humbled and despised.

When attacked by covetousness, understand that nothing but God can satisfy your heart, and recognize the folly of seeking anything but this supreme good.

In assaults against purity, reflect on how reception of the Holy Eucharist has raised your dignity. Think about the sacrilege you'd commit by profaning with carnal pleasures this temple God dwells in.

Against anger, defend yourself by saying, "No injury will move me to anger when I reflect upon the outrages I have done to God."

When assailed by temptations to hatred, say, "Knowing God's mercy and how He has pardoned my sins, I can't refuse to forgive my greatest enemy."

When attacked by gluttony, say, "I remember the vinegar

and gall the soldiers offered to Jesus on the cross, and I will blush if I don't deny my appetite for the expiation of my sins."

In temptations to sloth, arouse yourself to action by saying, "I can purchase eternal happiness by a few years of labor here below. I won't shrink from any toil for so great a reward."

Pride speaks with deceitful language, saying, "You excel others in learning, eloquence, wealth, rank, and many other things, so look down upon them." Humility answers, "Remember, you're dust and ashes, destined to become the food of worms."

Pride says, "Do all the good you can, but brag about it so the world may regard you as a person of great virtue and treat you with consideration and respect." Fear of God answers, "Don't pursue worldly renown at the cost of eternal glory. Hide your good actions, and if they appear in spite of your efforts to conceal them, God won't consider it vanity."

Hypocrisy counsels, "Assume the good qualities you don't possess, and make yourself appear better than you are." Sincerity answers, "It is better to be virtuous than to appear virtuous. By deceiving others, you cause your own ruin."

Rebellion and disobedience argue, "Don't subject yourself to authorities. You should command and they obey for they lack wisdom and virtue. It suffices to obey the laws of God." Submission and obedience answer, "The law of God obliges you to submit to people in authority."

Envy whispers, "You're better than those people others praise. You should enjoy the same or even greater adoration, for you excel them in many things." Brotherly love answers, "If your virtue exceeds that of others, keep it safe in obscurity, for the more you achieve, the greater the danger of falling. If the possessions of others equal or exceed yours, how does it harm you?" Remember that by envying others you become like those written of in Scripture when it says, "But by the envy of the devil, death entered the world, and they who are in his possession experience it." (Wis. 2:24)

Hatred says, "God can't oblige you to love someone who contradicts and opposes you, who continually speaks ill of you, ridicules you, reproaches you with your past failings, and thwarts you in everything." True Charity answers, "Despite someone's deplorable faults, we must never stop loving the image of God in them."

Jesus loved His enemies who nailed Him to the cross and He wants you to imitate His example. So drive from your heart the bitterness of hatred and yield to the sweetness of fraternal charity. Nothing provides greater sweetness than love or more bitterness than hatred that preys like a cancer on the heart.

Detraction exclaims, "You can't remain silent about the faults of such a bad person. To conceal their faults grants them approval to continue and renders you a participant as well." Charity answers, "Neither speak about your neighbor's sins nor participate in them but reprove him with mildness and patiently bear them. Moreover, wisdom sometimes ignores the faults of another until a favorable opportunity occurs for warning him against them."

Anger cries out, "How can you bear such affronts and so calmly submit to such injuries? If you don't fight back they'll insult you with impunity." Patience answers, "Reflect upon the ignominy Our Savior endured for you and you can bear any wrong with meekness." Remember also the words of St. Peter who said, "…Christ also suffered for you, leaving you an example that you should follow in His footsteps. When He was insulted, He returned no insult; when He suffered, He did not threaten…" (1Pet. 2:21, 23)

Hardness-of-heart urges, "It profits nothing to speak kindly to stupid, ignorant people who will probably presume upon your kindness and become insolent." Meekness answers, "Don't hold such thoughts, but heed the words of the Apostle: 'A slave of the Lord should not quarrel, but should be gentle with everyone…' (2Tim. 2:24) Inferiors must try with no less care to act with meekness and respect towards their superiors, and don't depend on the kindness of those in authority."

Presumption and imprudence argue, "God witnesses your actions and there's nothing wrong with them, so why do you care how they affect others?" Prudence answers, "You owe a duty of edification to your neighbor and your actions. Don't give him reason to suspect evil. Beware of scandalizing another, even with good acts others misunderstand. If your neighbor reproofs you correctly, humbly acknowledge your fault. If you've no guilt, proclaim your innocence with no less sincere humility."

Covetousness insinuates, "Don't share things with strangers but keep them for yourself." Mercy answers, "Remember the lesson of the covetous rich man of the Gospel who wore fine purple linen. God didn't condemn him for taking what didn't belong to him, but for not giving from his abundance. (Lk. 16:22) From the depth of hell, he begged for a drop of water to quench his thirst. But God denied him because he had refused the poor man at his gate even the crumbs that fell from his table."

Loquacity says, "It is no sin to talk much if you say no evil." Discreet reserve answers, "That is true but people who talk a lot seldom fail to offend others. Hence, the Bible teaches, 'Where words are many, sin is not wanting; but he who restrains his lips does well.' (Prov. 10:19) Moreover, if you avoid injurious words against your neighbor, you'll avoid many idle words for which you must render an account on the last day. Keep your speech moderate and reserved so your words don't entangle you in sin."

Impurity counsels, "Enjoy the pleasures life offers you, for you know not what may happen tomorrow. Enjoy the pleasures of youth, which passes like a dream. If God didn't want us to enjoy these pleasures, He wouldn't have created them." Chastity answers, "Don't let these illusions deceive you. Consider what God has prepared for you. If you live a pure life on earth, He'll reward you with eternal joy. However, if you abandon yourself to your impure desires, He'll punish you with torments equally unspeakable and eternal. The more you recognize the fleeting nature of these pleasures, the more earnestly you'll live chastely. Don't purchase an hour of gratification at the expense of endless suffering."

If you follow these counsels, you'll live virtuously and destroy your vices. You can defend your soul, the citadel God inhabits and leaves in your care. If you defend it resolutely and faithfully, you'll enjoy the love of this heavenly Guest, for the Apostle says, "…God is love, and whoever remains in love remains in God and God in him." (1 Jn. 4:16)

Chapter 40

The Three Kinds of Virtues in which the Fullness of Justice Consists; and First, Man's Duty to Himself

SECTION I
Our Threefold Obligation to Virtue

Now I'll focus on the virtues that elevate and adorn you with the spiritual treasures of justice. Justice requires you to render what is due God, your neighbor, and yourself. If you faithfully do this, you fulfill the obligations of justice and become truly virtuous. To accomplish this great work, treat God as your father, your neighbor as your brother, and yourself as a judge of yourself.

SECTION II
The Reformation of the Body

Charity begins at home. Therefore, control your body with all its organs and senses, and the soul with all its affections and powers. To perform this duty faithfully, establish an empire of virtue within yourself.

To reform the body and bring it under the dominion of virtue, acquire a modest and decorous bearing. St. Augustine said to have nothing about your manner or dress capable of scandalizing your neighbor, but practice pureness in everything. Hence, servants of God, bear yourselves with gravity, humility, and sweetness. This way everyone you meet may profit by your example and learn from your virtue. St. Paul urged Christians to be like fragrant plants, giving forth the sweet perfume of piety and filling all about with the odor of Jesus Christ. (2Cor. 2:15)

Exterior modesty helps you preserve the purity of your soul because they influence each other so strongly. For this reason, a composed and modest bearing contributes to interior calm and modesty, while a restless exterior upsets your soul.

The preceding remarks apply to manners in general. I shall next discuss modesty and sobriety at table.

SECTION III
Temperance

To reform your body, rigorously curb your appetites and refrain from immoderate indulgence of your senses. As the exceedingly bitter myrrh preserves the body from corruption after death, so mortifications preserve it during life from the corruption of vice. For this reason, sobriety provides the foundation for all virtues.

Holy Scripture teaches, "Behave at table like a favored guest, and be not greedy, lest you be despised. Be the first to stop, as befits good manners; gorge not yourself, lest you give offense. If there are many with you at table, be not the first to reach out your hand." (Sir: 31:16-18)

St. Bernard taught to regulate eating via time, manner, quantity, and quality. He urged to eat only during usual hours for eating, not to display eagerness, and not to eat more than others. (Ep. ad Fratres de Monte Dei.)

Though eating requires great prudence, drinking requires

even more, especially by the young. St. Jerome said that wine and youth provide two incentives to impurity. (Ad Eustoch, de Cust. Virg.) Wine is to youth what fuel is to fire. As oil poured upon the flames only increases their intensity, so wine, like a violent conflagration, heats the blood, enkindling and exciting passions to the highest pitch of folly and madness. This indulgence counteracts all moral virtues that subdue and control the baser passions. You need great vigilance to guard against the attacks of this enemy.

Remember that by wine I mean every kind of drink capable of robbing you of reason. A philosopher wisely said that the vine bears three kinds of grapes: necessity, pleasure, and folly. In other words, wine taken with moderation supports weakness, but beyond this limit it flatters the senses and drunk to excess, it produces madness.

Heed no inspiration or thought excited by wine. The worst of evil counselors, it produces unbridled tongues, immoderate laughter, vulgar jokes, violent disputes, the revelation of secrets, and many other unhappy consequences. Avoid with equal care all disputes or arguments at table, for they begin grave quarrels. Moderate both your speech and appetite.

Also, don't dwell on the merits of certain dishes and condemn others for their lack of delicacy. Don't fix your mind and heart on eating and drinking with such eagerness that the burden of your conversation focuses on the excellent fish of such a river, the luscious fruit of such a country, and the fine wines of such a region. This clearly proves you've lost sight of the true purpose of eating, which is to support nature. Thus, you debase your heart and intelligence and make them slaves to gluttony.

Let necessity, not pleasure, govern your eating and

drinking. Don't go hungry but never eat solely for pleasure.

SECTION IV
The Government of the Senses

Next, learn to govern your senses, especially the eyes through which death enters to rob your life. Without this guard, you can fall prey to vanities that you can't banish during prayer. Avoid images that tarnish the purity of your heart and turn your eyes away from curious objects and worldly vanities, so you can freely converse with God without distraction and advance spiritually.

The sense of hearing requires a no-less-vigilant guard, for through it you learn many things that weary, distract, and defile the soul. Protect your ears from evil words, frivolous conversations, worldly gossip, and idle discourses. During meditation, they can provide great obstacles to recollection and prayer.

SECTION V
The Government of the Tongue

Holy Scripture says, "Death and life are in the power of the tongue..." (Prov. 18:21) Thus, observe a just medium between silence and talkativeness, between timidity and self-sufficiency, between frivolity and pomposity. Always speak with gravity, moderation, sweetness, and simplicity. Beware of haughtily asserting and obstinately persisting in your statements, for this fault gives rise to disputes that wound charity and destroy the peace of the soul. Generously yield to contentions, and act as if ignorant and listen in silence.

Finally, consider the purpose of your words and don't speak to appear learned. Don't parade your wit and conversational powers as this promotes hypocrisy, deceit, self-love, and vanity. Direct all your conversation to a good end such as the glory of God or the profit of your neighbor.

Young people, defer your conversation in the presence of elders, the ignorant in the presence of the learned, and lay persons in the presence of ecclesiastics or religious. When you think your words may be untimely or presumptuous, remain silent. Not everyone can judge these situations correctly, so when in doubt, remain silent. For as Holy Scripture says, "Even a fool, if he keeps silent, is considered wise; if he closes his lips, intelligent." (Prov. 17:28)

SECTION VI
The Mortification of the Passions

Consider the sensual appetites that comprise all your natural affections such as love, hate, joy, sorrow, fear, hope, anger, and other sentiments of like nature. These appetites comprise the inferior part of the soul, which gives you your strongest resemblance to irrational animals who survive by instinct. Nothing degrades you more or leads you further from God than to act like them.

Your sensual appetites, like an arsenal, provide sin with the most dangerous weapons. In this vulnerable part of your soul, a second Eve, frail and inconstant, surrenders to the wiles of the old serpent. When she falls, she drags with her the unhappy Adam, the superior part of your soul, the seat of the will and understanding. Here, original sin manifests in all its power and concentrates its poison. On this field of battle, defeats and victories occur, so exercise virtue and fight. Use all your courage and merit to overcome the blind passions that spring from your sensual appetites.

Theologians often represent a soul as a vine needing careful pruning or as a garden that needs weeding to remove the vices to make room for the virtuous plants. Cultivate your garden as the principal occupation of your life and ruthlessly pluck from your soul all that chokes the growth of good. Then you'll become a true child of God, guided by the Holy Spirit, and live as a spiritual being. You'll follow the guidance of grace and the dictates of reason and not behave like a carnal beast obeying the impulses of passion.

Carefully study your dispositions and inclinations and most vigilantly guard the weakest part of your nature. Wage constant war against your appetites, and pay particular attention to combating the desire of honors, riches, and pleasures, for these are the roots of all evils.

Beware of pride, especially if you hold a position of authority. To conquer it, learn to deny yourself innocent gratifications and to bear contradictions with dignity and patience. Humble yourself by doing lowly and obscure things. Don't worry about opinions of others, for they can't take or give you anything because your inheritance comes only from God.

SECTION VII
The Reformation of the Will

Humility of heart, poverty of spirit, and a holy hatred of self provide the most effective ways to achieve the reformation of the will. St. Bernard taught that humility comes from a true understanding of your baseness. This virtue plucks from your heart all the roots of pride as well as all love of earthly honors and dignities. It inspires you to seek the lowest place, persuading you that if another had received the graces you enjoy, they'd have shown more gratitude and used them more profitably for the glory of God. Finally, while maintaining your dignity, always submit to superiors, equals, and inferiors for the love of God.

Poverty of spirit consists in a voluntary contempt for the things of this world and perfect contentment with where God has placed you, however poor and lowly. This virtue destroys love of wealth and provides great peace and contentment. Because all misery springs from unfulfilled desires, you approach very near the summit of happiness when you learn to subdue your desires.

Holy hatred of self means to subject yourself to reason and deny yourself inordinate desires so you can help your soul. It doesn't mean to yield to despair, but recognize that many evils come from the flesh and block your path to goodness. Hatred of self provides your chief instrument in the work of salvation. It enables you to uproot and cast out evil inclinations.

SECTION VIII
The Government of the Imagination

Imagination and understanding also belong to the sensual appetites. Original sin impacted imagination greatly and makes it hard for reason to control. Continually escaping vigilance, like a restless child it runs hither and thither, sometimes flying to the remotest corners of the world before you realize it. It eagerly seizes things that allure it. If you don't control it, but rather indulge its caprices like a spoiled child, you'll strengthen its evil tendencies. Then when you wish to pray, you'll vainly seek to restrain it and it will rebel against you.

Knowing the dangerous propensities of this power, vigilantly guard it and cut off all unprofitable reflections. To do this, carefully examine your thoughts and select which to indulge and which to reject. If not careful, ideas and sentiments will penetrate your heart and weaken devotion, diminish fervor, and destroy charity.

SECTION IX
The Government of the Understanding

Understanding raises you above all creatures and makes you most resemble God. The beauty of this power depends upon that rare virtue, prudence. In the spiritual life, prudence is to the soul what the eyes are to the body.

To lead a virtuous life, let prudence guide you in all things. Not limited to any special duty, it enters into the fulfillment of all duties, into the practice of all virtues, and preserves order and harmony among them. Prudence directs all your actions to God.

Guide your interactions with your neighbors with prudence so you can enlighten and not scandalize them. Observe the condition and character of others, so that you may wisely benefit them, patiently bearing with their failings and closing your eyes to infirmities that you can't cure.

"Wise people don't," said Aristotle, "expect the same degree of certainty in all things; some things remain obscure, others readily apparent. Moreover, don't expect the same degree of perfection from everyone, for some can achieve perfections others can't. Therefore, whoever forces everyone to the same standard of virtue does more harm than good."

Prudence teaches how to recognize your inclinations, failings, and evil tendencies. Prudence also guards you against the error of opening your mind to all you meet, or of making confidants of others without due reflection. By putting a just restraint upon your words, it saves you from too freely expressing your opinion and thereby committing many faults.

Whenever you expect to transact business with people who easily anger, or to encounter any danger, try to foresee the perils of the occasion and arm yourself against them.

Prudence also requires moderation in all your works, even the holiest, and to preserve you from exhausting the spirit by indiscreet labor. Don't let your work cause you to lose sight of interior duties, nor devotion to your neighbor make you forget what you owe God.

Finally, prudence teaches about the snares of the enemy by counseling: "...test the spirits to see whether they belong to God, because many false prophets have gone out into the world. And no wonder, for even the devil masquerades as an angel of light." (1Jn. 4:1 and 2Cor. 11:14) Fear most the temptation that presents itself under the mask of virtue, for the devil frequently employs this method to deceive pious souls. Inspired and guided by prudence, recognize these snares and let fear keep you from danger but animated by a holy courage to win every battle. Avoid extremes and prevent your neighbor from suffering scandal, but remain undaunted by groundless fears. Learn to despise the opinions of the world and don't fear its outcries against virtue. Remember St. Paul's advice that if you please people, you can't be a servant of Jesus Christ. (Gal. 1:10)

SECTION X
Prudence in Temporal Affairs

Prudence also provides great help with temporal affairs by saving you from both minor and serious problems, either material or spiritual. Thus, prudence suggests you look at a planned project and enter it carefully. Begin with prayer, then weigh all its circumstances and consequences that might likely flow from it. Next, seek wise counsel and deliberate upon the advice you receive. Finally, reflect upon all you've learned before acting.

Beware of the four great enemies of prudence: hastiness, passion, obstinate persistence in your own opinions, and vanity. Hastiness accepts no reasoning, passion blinds, obstinacy turns a deaf ear to all counsel, and vanity ruins everything.

Prudence seeks a just middle ground in all things. Don't let the faults of a few lead you to condemn the many, or the virtues of a few make you believe in the piety of all. Follow the guidance of reason in all things and don't hurry to extremes. This failing disposes you favorably towards the old and makes you dislike the new. Prudence guards against this, for age can no more justify the bad than novelty can condemn the good. Don't esteem things for their age, but for their merit. A long-standing vice is difficult to eradicate, and a virtue of recent growth has the fault of being unknown.

Thoroughly know that reflection and gravity remain inseparable companions of prudence, and rashness and levity always accompany folly. Therefore, don't believe everything you hear, for this indicates levity of mind, and don't make promises that bind you beyond your means.

SECTION XI
Means of Acquiring this Virtue

Failure and the experience of others provide wise lessons about prudence. But humility provides an even better way to learn because pride is the greatest obstacle to this virtue. "When pride comes, disgrace comes; but with the humble is wisdom." (Prov. 11:2)

Humility doesn't require you to yield blindly to all opinions or indiscreetly follow every counsel. This isn't humility but weakness and instability. Resolutely maintain the truth and vigorously support justice. Don't allow contrary opinions to carry you away.

Finally, devout and humble prayer provides powerful aid in acquiring the virtue of prudence, for the Holy Spirit wants to enlighten you with the gifts of knowledge, wisdom, and counsel. The greater your humility and devotion with which you present yourself before God, the greater the graces you shall receive.

Chapter 41

Man's Duty to His Neighbor

Your duty toward your neighbor includes charity and mercy. Read Holy Scriptures and you'll appreciate the importance of these virtues. The writings of the prophets, Apostles, and evangelists abound with counsels concerning them. St. John frequently mentions the importance of charity. So frequently did he repeat to his disciples the touching words, "My little children, love one another," that at last, as St. Jerome says, they became somewhat weary of always hearing the same, and asked him,: "Good master, why do you always give this one command?" To which he replied, "Because it is the command of the Lord and if you do this alone it will suffice." (De Scriptoribus Eccles.) Thus, to please God, fulfill this great precept of charity in word and deed. Among the works of charity, pay particular attention to advice, counsel, succor, forbearance, pardon, and edification. These so strongly link to charity that the practice of them indicates the progress you've made in the practice of charity.

Some Christians pretend to love their neighbor, but their charity goes no further than words. Others give advice, but offer no more substantial proof of their charity. Others will perform both these duties, but resent injury, or refuse to bear with the infirmities of their neighbor, forgetting that the Apostle says, "Bear one another's burdens, and so you will fulfill the law of Christ." (Gal. 6:2)

Others, while not resenting an injury, continue to harbor it deep within and won't freely pardon it. Finally, many fulfill all these obligations, yet in their words or conduct fail to give their neighbor that edification, the most important duty of charity. Diligently examine your hearts and actions and determine how well you fulfill the precepts of this virtue.

If you love your neighbor, you possess the first degree of charity. If you give them good counsel, you achieve the second. If you help them with poverty or distress, you attain the third degree. If you patiently bear an injury, you possess the fourth. If you can freely pardon it, you attain the fifth degree. Finally, in addition to all this, if you can edify your neighbor, you'll have attained the highest degree of charity.

These comprise the positive acts of charity, but negative duties exist as well. Avoid rash judgments, speaking evil, using abusive or insulting language, injuring honor or reputation, and promoting scandal by word or evil counsel.

Love your neighbor like a mother loves her children. See with what devotion a good mother cares for her children. How prudently she counsels them in danger, helps them, and sacrifices herself for them. You'd have perfect charity if you do this for your neighbor. Though you may not attain this degree, nevertheless aspire to it.

You'll doubtless think that you can't feel such affection for a stranger. However, don't regard your neighbor as a stranger but rather as the image of God, the work of His divine hands, and a living member of Christ. Paul taught that when you sin against your neighbor you sin against Christ. (1Cor. 8:12) Look on your neighbor not as a person but as

Christ Himself, for Christ assures He considers as done to Him all that you do to your neighbor.

But, above all, ever keep before your eyes the incomparable example of Our Savior's love. He loved us with so much tenderness, devotion, and generosity to encourage us by His example. On the night before He suffered, He gave his parting words to His Apostles. "I give you a new commandment: love one another. As I have loved you..." (Jn. 13:34)

Chapter 42

Man's Duty to God

SECTION I
Man's Duties in General

The third and noblest obligation of justice comprises man's duty to God, which includes the practice of the theological virtues, faith, hope, and charity, and of the virtue called religion, which has for its object the worship due to God.

To love God with the affection of a dutiful child provides the most secure way of fulfilling this obligation. Consider how a good son manifests his love for his father; how great is his devotion, his fear, his reverence for him. How faithfully he obeys him and zealously and disinterestedly serves him. With what confidence he goes to him in all his necessities and with what submission he accepts his corrections. Serve God with such a heart and you'll faithfully fulfill this obligation of justice.

To attain this you'll require love, holy fear, confidence, zeal for the glory of God, purity of intention, the spirit of prayer, gratitude, conformity to the will of God, humility, and patience in tribulation.

SECTION II
The Love of God

First, love God, as He commanded, with your whole heart, with your whole soul, and with your whole strength. (Deut. 6:5) All your faculties must cooperate in loving and serving this great Master.

SECTION III
The Fear of God

Fear springs from love and the greater your love for another, the greater you'll fear losing or offending God. See how carefully a good son avoids anything that could displease his father, or a loving wife, all that could displease her husband. This fear guards your innocence, so deeply engrave it in your soul, praying with David that the Lord may pierce your flesh with His holy fear.

SECTION IV
Confidence in God

To fear add confidence. Like a child who fears no danger in his father's protecting arms, place yourself into the arms of your Heavenly Father, confident that those Hands that sustain the heavens will supply your necessities, uphold you in temptation, and turn all things to your profit.

When you cross a rapid stream and the turbulent waters make you dizzy, instead of looking down at the torrent, you look above to restore your steadiness. Do likewise when afraid and don't dwell upon your unworthiness or your failings, but raise your eyes to God and consider the infinite goodness and mercy He wants to apply to your miseries. Reflect upon His truthfulness and His promise to help and comfort all who humbly and confidently invoke His sacred name. Consider also the innumerable benefits you've already received from God and let this inspire you to trust the future to Him with renewed hope.

SECTION V
Zeal for the Glory of God

Zeal consists in promoting the honor of God and striving to advance the fulfillment of His will on earth. If you love God, you can't but fill with grief to see so many neglecting to obey His holy will.

SECTION VI
Purity of Intention

This virtue, intimately connected with zeal, enables you to forget yourself in all things, and to seek first the glory of God and the accomplishment of His good pleasure. You'll realize that the more you sacrifice your own interests in His service, the greater advantage and blessing you'll reap. But examine your motives to ensure you labor purely for God and not for self-love, which insinuates itself into every work unless you maintain a constant guard. For the lack of this pure intention, God will find many who seem rich in good works very poor on judgment day.

People in high positions can lead irreproachable lives, carefully avoiding anything unbecoming the dignity of their station, but with bad motives. They see that virtue promotes their position, and consequently they practice it in a manner that secures advancement to greater dignities. Thus, they don't fear or love God or have obedience to His divine will, but to their own interest. Such virtue may deceive people, but God sees it as smoke and only the shadow of justice.

You can attain this virtue only with difficulty so earnestly ask it of God, especially in the Lord's Prayer. Frequently repeat with fervor, "Thy will be done on earth, as it is in Heaven." Beg Him to grant you the grace to imitate on earth the purity and devotion with which the heavenly choirs bless and fulfill His adorable will.

SECTION VII
Prayer

I urge you to turn to God in childlike prayer whenever afflictions or temptations come upon you and you'll preserve a continual recollection of God. You'll live in His presence and His love will abide in your heart. Prayer enables you most faithfully and frequently to testify your reverence and love for God.

SECTION VIII
Gratitude

Hold the virtue of gratitude in your heart and let it motivate you to praise God unceasingly for continuously preserving, protecting, and lavishing blessings on you.

Begin all your tasks by giving thanks. St. Basil said to make it the beginning of all prayers. Morning and evening and at all times, give thanks to God for His many benefits, general and particular, but above all, for the incomprehensible benefits of redemption and the Blessed Sacrament. Remember, in all these blessings, He sought only your welfare.

SECTION IX
Obedience

The virtue of obedience makes you most pleasing to God, for it embraces the perfection of justice. This virtue includes obedience to the commandments, counsels, and inspirations of God. You must obey the commandments to achieve salvation. Obeying God's counsels facilitates the observance of the commandments and obeying divine inspirations enables you to accept with equal submission, honor or ignominy, obscurity or renown, stripes or caresses, health or sickness, and life or death. In your chastisements, know that He inflicts them with love. An earthly father loves his child when he corrects him no less than when he caresses him and God works the same way. Realize that all that comes from His hand comes for your benefit and you'll become so firmly established in submission to His Holy Will that He'll mold you according to His good pleasure, as clay in the hands of a potter.

Thus you'll no longer live for yourself, but for God. You'll find happiness only in accomplishing His divine will, in doing all things, in bearing all things for His glory, and acting at all times as His submissive servant.

Don't forget that this submission to God, and this promptness in obeying Him, must rely on prudence and judgment, so that you don't mistake your own will for that of God. In most cases, distrust what flatters your inclinations, and proceed with more confidence when you act contrary to your personal interests.

God, in His infinite goodness, wants to overwhelm you with His graces when you offer no obstacle to His merciful designs. Whoever obeys His will can justly expect an abundance of His favors. Yes, God will treat you with great liberality, and will make you like another David, the apple of His eye.

SECTION X
Patience in Afflictions

Suffering patiently provides the key to achieving obedience to God's will. Solomon wrote, "My son, …disdain not; spurn not his reproof; for whom He loves, he reproves, and he chastises the son he favors." (Prov. 3:11-12)

Since a good father corrects and disciplines his children, good children must patiently endure the correction and accept it as a proof of their father's love. Jesus taught this lesson when He said to St. Peter, "…Shall I not drink the cup that the Father gave me?" (Jn. 18:11) If the chalice of suffering came to you by another hand, you might justly refuse it. However, knowing that your loving Father sent it allows you to accept it without hesitation. Nevertheless, many Christians, perfectly conformed to Divine Will in prosperity, abandon Him when adversity approaches. Like cowards, they vaunt their courage in time of peace, but throw down their arms and fly at the first sound of battle. Life has many combats and trials, so strengthen your soul with salutary reflections and when the hour of conflict arrives, submit perfectly to His Divine Will.

Chapter 43

The Obligations of our State

Duties vary according to your station in life. For example, leaders have different duties from followers and the duties of a religious differ greatly from those of a parent.

Virtue requires following orders willingly and submitting your judgment to your superiors. Many fulfill the commands of a superior, but with reluctance, others obey but murmur and disapprove the command. Others cheerfully obey and heartily approve whatever order they receive.

Strive for obedience by remembering when Jesus said, "Whoever listens to you listens to me. Whoever rejects you rejects me. And whoever rejects me rejects the one who sent me." (Lk. 10:16) Refrain from all murmuring against superiors, so you don't deserve the reproach addressed by Moses to the Israelites: "Your grumbling is not against us, but against the Lord." (Exod. 16:8)

Married women, faithfully do your duties and practice piety without neglecting your family.

Fathers, don't neglect chastising your children. Remember, the sins of children, to a certain degree, come from bad parents. You don't deserve the title father if you fail to train your children for this world or prepare them for the kingdom of Heaven. Guard them from evil associates, give them wise and virtuous masters, and teach them to love virtue.

Don't gratify their whims, but curb their wills that they may learn submissiveness. Provide for both their spiritual and corporal wants. Fulfill the duties of a father in a manner becoming a Christian, a true servant of God, and you'll make your children heirs to Heaven, and not slaves of Hell.

Chapter 44

The Relative Importance and Values of the Virtues

When people purchase precious stones, they need to know the value of each one. In like manner, you need to know the value of each virtue to make proper choices. To help with this, I divide virtues into two groups, interior spiritual virtues and exterior sensible virtues.

I place the three theological virtues in the interior spiritual group because they focus on God. They also include the virtues that help you accomplish your duty to God, such as humility, chastity, mercy, patience, prudence, devotion, poverty of spirit, contempt of the world, denial of your will, love of the cross, mortification, and many others.

The exterior virtues, or sensible virtues, include fasting, mortification, pious reading, vocal prayer, chanting of Psalms, pilgrimages, attending Mass, assisting at the offices of the Church, and all outward ceremonies and practices of Christian life. Though these virtues reside in the soul, they always act exteriorly.

The virtues of the first group please God more than those of the second group. We know this because Jesus said to the woman at the well, "Believe me, woman, the hour is coming when you will worship the Father neither on this mountain or in Jerusalem. But the hour is coming, and is now here, when true worshippers will worship the Father in Spirit and truth." (Jn. 4:21, 23-24)

However, don't conclude that the others have no value. Though not so noble as the former, they help acquire and preserve them. For example, retreat and solitude guard against innumerable sights and sounds that endanger the peace of your conscience and imperil your chastity. Fasting while in a state of grace expiates your sins, subdues the inclinations of the flesh, repels your enemy, disposes you to prayer, and preserves you from passions. Pious reading, the recitation of the Psalms, assisting at the Divine Office, and hearing sermons enlighten you and make you desire spiritual things. Thus, strive for the interior virtues by practicing the exterior virtues. The first group represent the health of your body and the second, the medicine to attain it.

By practicing both interior and exterior virtues, you can avoid two equally lamentable errors, one made by the Pharisees in the time of Christ and the other by non-believers today. The Pharisees were carnal, ambitious, and accustomed to the literal observance of the law, disregarded true justice and interior virtues. They concealed their corrupt and wicked hearts under a virtuous exterior. The non-believers of today, trying to avoid this error, go to the opposite extreme and have contempt for exterior practices. However, the Catholic Church preserves a happy medium between both and, while maintaining the superiority of the interior virtues, recognizes the merit and advantage of the exterior.

Chapter 45

Four Important Corollaries of the Preceding Doctrine

SECTION I
The Necessity of Exterior as well as Interior Virtues

A true servant of God must practice exterior virtues to preserve interior virtues and to fulfill the obligations of justice. Neither the soul without the body nor the body without the soul constitutes completeness.

SECTION II
Discernment in the Pursuit of Virtue

As people will pay more for gold than silver, it takes more effort to acquire the greater virtues than the lesser virtues.

Others can see your exterior faults, so you likely consider them more important than interior defects and thus work harder to correct them. Don't fall into this trap. Moreover, the exterior virtues bring more esteem than the practice of hope, charity, humility, and fear of God or contempt for the world.

SECTION III
Lesser virtues must sometimes yield to greater virtues.

When forced to choose between two commandments, follow the more important one. Observe the same rule with regard to virtues. Whenever unsure about which to choose, choose the greater. St. Bernard said that the Holy Fathers established many practices to preserve and increase charity. When these practices work well, follow them, but if they conflict with charity, modify them.

SECTION IV
True and False Justice

There are two types of justice, false and true. True justice embraces both the interior and the exterior virtues. False justice needs only a few exterior practices, while neglecting the interior virtues, such as love of God, humility, and devotion. This was the justice of the Pharisees, to whom Jesus addressed these terrible words, "Woe to you, scribes and Pharisees, you hypocrites. You pay tithes of mint and dill and cumin, and have neglected the weightier things of the law: judgment and mercy and fidelity. (But) these you should have done, without neglecting the others. Woe to you, scribes and Pharisees, you hypocrites. You cleanse the outside of cup and dish, but inside they are full of plunder and self-indulgence. Blind Pharisee, cleanse first the inside of the cup, so that the outside also may be clean. Woe to you, scribes and Pharisees, you hypocrites. You are like whitewashed tombs, which appear beautiful on the outside, but inside are full of dead men's bones and every kind of filth." (Matt. 23:23,25,27) Scripture frequently condemns this type of justice.

Chapter 46

The Different Vocations in the Church

A good Christian usually doesn't practice all the virtues with the same ardor. Some prefer to cultivate the virtues that focus on God and therefore embrace a contemplative life. Others prefer the virtues that enable them to help their neighbor, and consequently choose an active life. Others prefer the virtues that more directly benefit their own souls, and therefore enter the monastic life. Again, as all virtues provide means for acquiring grace, different persons adopt different ones. Many seek to obtain it by fasting and other austerities, others by almsgiving and works of mercy, and others by prayer and meditation.

Beware of a grave error into which pious persons sometimes fall. Deriving much profit from certain means, many imagine they've found the only path to God. Consequently, they want to enforce the same method upon everyone and think all in error who follow a different path. Thus, one who focuses wholly on prayer thinks it the only means of salvation. Another, given to fasting and corporal mortification, sees no merit in any other practices of piety. Those who lead contemplative lives imagine that all who engage in an active life remain in great danger, and even go so far as to hold exterior virtues in contempt.

The followers of the active life, having no experience of all that passes between God and the soul in the sweet calm of contemplation, often don't sufficiently appreciate its value. They approve it only as far as it includes the practice of exterior works. One who gives himself exclusively to mental prayer will likely think any other form of prayer unprofitable. Conversely, those who devote themselves to vocal prayer often argue that it provides more merit because of its difficulty. Thus, impelled by ignorance or unconscious pride, many only recommend the practices they like the best and depreciate the merit of all others.

Seriously weigh these considerations and respect all vocations. Don't reproach the hand for not being the foot, nor the foot for not being the hand. Understand the truth of the Apostle's words when he taught that the beauty and perfection of the body result from the diversity of its members.

Chapter 47

The Vigilance and Care Necessary in the Practice of Virtue

Since my rules of life contain so many aspects, you'll need to focus your efforts. Practice one virtue that addresses all of them. Such is the virtue of continual vigilance in all your words and actions.

An ambassador about to address a world leader studies what to say, how to say it, and what gestures to use. As a Christian and an ambassador of the faith, speak carefully at all times, whether you speak with family, friends, business associates, or even in silent prayer. Measure all your actions and words by the law of the Divine Master.

Sacred Scripture recommends this virtue when it says, "However, take care and be earnestly on your guard..." (Deut. 4:9) and "...walk humbly with your God." (Mich. 6:8) That is, be careful to avoid everything contrary to His will.

Besides the many dangers that try to ensnare you, the difficulty and delicacy of the work of salvation makes vigilance indispensable, particularly if you aspire to the perfection of the spiritual life. To live in union with God while avoiding corruption requires grace and vigilance. Follow in this respect the wise counsel of Seneca who said to imagine yourself always in the presence of someone you greatly respect, and refrain from all that you'd not do in their presence. (Epist. 25)

Live each day as if it were your last, and in the evening give God an account of all your actions. Another effective approach requires you to walk continually in the presence of God and to act in all things with obedience due to so great a Master. Frequently implore His grace to avoid all that makes you unworthy of His divine presence.

Thus, vigilance has two goals. First, to fix the eyes of your soul upon God and unceasingly offer Him on the altar of your heart a sacrifice of adoration, respect, praise, devotion, thanksgiving, and love. Secondly, watch over all your thoughts, words, and actions, so that in all things you may follow the guidance of His will. Though you'll not achieve these goals easily, strive for them always.

Chapter 48

The Courage necessary in the Practice of Virtue

SECTION I

The Necessity of Courage

Vigilance and courage can overcome two main obstacles: discerning good from evil and choosing good over evil. Vigilance addresses the first and fortitude the second. These two indispensable virtues provide the key, for without vigilance you're blind, craven and helpless.

By courage, I don't mean the cardinal virtue of fortitude that calms your fears and strengthens you in affliction, but rather the disposition of the soul that enables you to triumph over all obstacles to good. For this reason, it ever accompanies virtue, sword in hand to vanquish all her foes.

As the blacksmith requires a hammer to beat the hard iron and shape it according to his will, so do you need courage, the spiritual hammer, with which to overcome the difficulties in the road to virtue and fashion your soul after God. Without this quality, you can no more pursue virtue than a blacksmith can work without a hammer.

You can't acquire this virtue without effort. Consider prayer, fasting, temperance, obedience, poverty of spirit, chastity, humility and you'll find that all present some difficulty springing from self-love, the world, or the devil. Therefore, if you sincerely desire to advance in virtue, consider the words spoken to Moses by God as directly addressed to you. "Take this staff in your hand; with it you are to perform the signs that will deliver My people." (Ex. 4:17) Rest assured that as that rod enabled Moses to deliver the children of Israel, so the rod of courage will enable you to work no less striking wonders. Keep this rod, therefore, ever in your hand, for without it you'll remain utterly helpless.

Also, avoid an illusion that beginners in the spiritual life frequently fall prey to. Having read in certain books of the ineffable consolations of the Holy Spirit and the joys of God's service, they persuade themselves that delights fill the path of virtue, so instead of entering it armed to meet their enemies, they set out as if for a festival. Truly, the love of God is full of sweetness, but the way that leads to it contains much bitterness, because you must first conquer self-love, the most difficult opponent to defeat.

God favors with ineffable consolations souls who faithfully labor for Him and renounce the pleasures of the world for those of Heaven. He requires absolute renunciation because if you refuse to sacrifice the joys of this life you vainly seek the joys of the Holy Spirit.

If you don't arm yourself with courage, your pursuit of virtue will fail. You attain rest through labor, victory through combat, joy through tears, and God's love through hatred of self. For this reason, the Holy Spirit, throughout the Proverbs of Solomon, so frequently condemns sloth and negligence and so strongly commends vigilance and courage as the safeguards of virtue.

SECTION II
Means of acquiring Courage

It takes courage to practice virtue because it helps you acquire all other virtues. However, you will likely find it difficult to acquire. Some find it so difficult they cower and flee. However, you can stimulate your courage by contemplating the fortitude of the many Christians who cheerfully embraced poverty, mortification, and humiliations for love of Christ. Many of them so loved suffering for Christ that they sought it as eagerly as many seek pleasure, gain, and riches. The Church daily presents such heroic souls so you can both honor and imitate them.

Also consider the courage and heroism of the martyrs who endured all types of hideous tortures, some burned alive and others wild beasts tore to pieces. Many had their flesh torn from their bodies with red-hot pincers. Some died in caldrons of boiling oil. Others had to walk barefoot on burning coals. Some suffered while tied to the tails of wild horses and dragged through thickets and briars. An executioner in Nicodemia scourged a martyr so cruelly that every blow brought away a piece of his flesh, leaving his bones exposed, and into these cruel wounds he poured salt and vinegar. Then finding that his victim remained alive, the executioner placed the body of his victim upon a slow fire, turning it from side to side with iron hooks until his soul took flight to God. Read the lives of those brave soldiers of Christ and your courage will increase and you'll grow ashamed of the little you've done for God.

They were human like you and their bodies felt pain just like yours. They had the same God to assist them and they hoped for the same heavenly reward. Since eternal life cost them so much, never refuse to sacrifice to attain this blessed end. Have the courage to fast one day when you see people dying of hunger. Don't refuse to remain for a short time on your knees in prayer, knowing they continued to pray for their enemies during long hours of agony. Resist your inclinations and passions, knowing they unhesitatingly abandoned their bodies to the tortures of the executioner. They endured without murmuring the solitude and suffering of dark prisons, so don't refuse your soul a few moments of solitude in prayer each day to amend your past and to prepare for your future. If these examples don't move you, lift your eyes to the cross and contemplate Jesus who hangs there in torment for love of you. May these considerations reanimate your courage and stimulate you to follow these bright examples.

Let me conclude this work with the words of Our Savior: "If anyone wishes to come after me, he must deny himself and take up his cross daily and follow me." (Lk. 9:23) In this brief counsel, you find a summary of His divine doctrine and the secret of attaining the perfection taught in the Gospel. Thus, while your body may fall prey to hardships and labors, your soul will enjoy a paradise of peace, and this interior sweetness will enable you cheerfully to embrace all sufferings.

Abandonment to Divine Providence
by
Fr. Jean-Pierre de Caussade, SJ

"Today, listen to the voice of the Lord:
Do not grow stubborn, as your fathers did
in the wilderness, when at Meriba and Massah
they challenged and provoked me,
Although they had seen all my works."

Psalm 95

A Note from Brother Bob

Quite likely, you're presently experiencing a difficulty in y our life and you can't understand the reason. If you read the next thirty pages of this book by Father Jean-Pierre de Caussade, you may be able to better understand what is happening to you and why.

Chapter 1

The Same Now as Then

God speaks to us today just as He spoke to people in Biblical times. In those days, spirituality consisted of faithfulness to God with little spiritual guidance. Today, we have the help of the Church, the writings of saints, and our pastors and deacons to help us understand. Perhaps our present difficulties make this necessary, but the simple and straightforward souls of early times didn't have these resources. Then, for those who led a spiritual life, each moment brought some duty from God to accomplish. Their whole attention moved like a clock hand, marking time minute by minute. Their minds, continuously animated by divine grace, turned to each new duty God presented throughout the day.

Mary, the most humble and closely united person to God, demonstrated this when she responded to the Angel Gabriel when he told her that she'd be the mother of Christ. She radiated fundamental submission to the will of God when she replied, "Behold the handmaid of the Lord. May it be done to me according to your word."

At this moment, God required great faith from Mary. She recognized the magnificence of this event as the fulfillment of God's will. Whether she performed ordinary or extraordinary tasks, she knew they revealed God's will and provided ways to glorify Him. Her spirit, transported with joy, looked upon all that she did or suffered at each moment as a gift from God.

She knew that God fills the hearts with good things for those who hunger and thirst for Him rather than the things of this world. Mary showed us what we should always hold in our hearts.

The Bible contains very few details about the ordinary and simple life of the most Holy Virgin, but we know that she suffered and did the same things as anyone living in that time and place. She visited her cousin, Elizabeth, she took shelter in a stable with Joseph and the baby Jesus, she returned to Nazareth and lived with Jesus and Joseph, and they supported themselves by the work of their hands.

However, Divine treasures of grace filled their lives moment to moment via the most ordinary events. Such moments happen to us as well. God gave them and continues to give us these blessings of the present moment. God reveals Himself to the humble in the simplest ways. Thus, we see a basic and fundamental concept of Abandonment to Divine Providence.

Sometimes life presents difficult and apparently insurmountable difficulties. However, they only appear so because we don't view the situation correctly. We must approach all such things by actively or passively accepting them as coming from God at the very moment they arrive.

The active practice of accepting them consists in doing these new necessary tasks promptly and to the best of our ability. The passive practice consists in lovingly believing that God sends them as gifts moment by moment to lead us to perfection.

Quick now, make your fortune for eternity. Accept all things as a beautiful bouquet from Jesus that he wishes to share with you.

St. Mary Magdelen de Pazzi

Chapter 2

He's Always Present

By faith we know God holds all creatures in His hands. We know that all things live through Jesus Christ and that His divine operations will continue until the end of time, embracing each passing moment and the smallest atom's mysterious actions.

After the Resurrection, Jesus Christ surprised His disciples with various disguised appearances. This same Jesus, ever living, ever working, still takes people by surprise. At all times, God presents Himself under the cover of some pain, joy, or duty to perform. All that takes place within us, around us, or through us, contains and conceals His divine actions.

He is really, truly, and invisibly present at all times and places. This surprises us because we often don't recognize His operation at all or until later if we take the time to think about it. However, if we learn to lift the veil, open our eyes, and focus our attention, we will continually see Him reveal Himself and see His divine action in everything that happens to us. At each successive occurrence, we learn to say, "It is the Lord." Once we understand this, we begin to accept every fresh circumstance as a gift from God.

If we live such a life of faith, we can have an ongoing and constant familiar dialogue with Him. Then we will find ourselves doing everything for God and see all events as excellent and holy.

Whether human beings, vegetables or cosmic dust we all dance to a mysterious tune intoned in the distance by an invisible player.

Albert Einstein

Chapter 3

Believe to See

Someone enlightened by faith judges things very differently than someone having only natural senses to measure them, and can see the incredible treasures they contain. Faithful people know that the more repulsive something appears, the more clearly it contains God's divine operation.

Someone who knows that a certain person in disguise is an important person, treats him very differently than someone who thinks he's just an ordinary person. In the same way, the person who sees the will of God in every small event, especially those most distressing, receives all things with equal joy, pleasure and respect. They open all their doors to receive with honor what others fear and fly from with horror. The outward appearance may be mean and contemptible, but beneath this disguise, the heart discovers and honors the majesty of the Lord.

The more disturbing His entry in such a disguise, the more our hearts should fill with love. I cannot describe what the heart feels when it accepts the divine will in such humble, poor, and mean disguises. Imagine how the sight of God, poor and humble, lodged in a stable, lying on straw, weeping and trembling, pierced the loving heart of Mary! Ask the inhabitants of Bethlehem what they thought of the Child. You know what answer they gave and how they would have honored Him had He lodged in a palace surrounded by royalty.

Then ask Mary and Joseph, the Magi and the Shepherds. They will tell you that they found in this extreme poverty an indescribable tenderness, and an infinite dignity worthy of the majesty of God. Things that escape our normal senses strengthen and increase our faith. The less we see, the more we believe.

To adore Jesus on the Cross and to accept the will of God in extraordinary circumstances forms the basis of our faith. But those with even greater faith adore God in ordinary things. And when in faith they triumph over every effort to destroy it, they obtain a more glorious victory. To consider God equally good in small and ordinary things as in great and uncommon things requires not ordinary faith, but great and extraordinary faith.

We can never have too much confidence in our good God who is so powerful and so merciful. We obtain from him as much as we hope for.

St. Therese The Little Flower

Chapter 4

Abandon Yourself to Him

A most loving aspect of these gifts, especially the difficult ones, is that none of them require strength we don't have. God never sends anything we can't handle. For example, we all need to attend Mass every Sunday but if sickness prevents us we don't have to go. The same rule holds good for all the teachings of the Church. Only those which forbid evil things remain absolute, because the Church always forbids sin. This is wonderfully reasonable. God only requires us to do what He has given us the strength to accomplish. He requires it from both high and low, from the strong and the weak, in a word from all, always and everywhere moment to moment.

He requires only simple and easy things to attain holiness. His moment-to-moment gifts to us always match our skills and character and this makes them easy. He never impels anyone beyond his strength or aptitude because He is a kind and loving parent.

Take delight and satisfaction in the present moment and adore the divine will in all you do or suffer. People with strong faith adore God with redoubled love and respect in each difficult or happy situation. Nothing hides Him from piercing eyes of faith. The louder the senses proclaim there is no God in this bad thing, the more firmly they embrace their "bundle of myrrh." Nothing daunts them, and nothing disgusts them.

The designs of God, the good pleasure of God, the will of God, the operation of God and the gift of His grace are all one and the same. He works in our souls to make us like Him. We become like Him by faithfully cooperating with Him. This cooperation creates a divine state within us like medicine that cures a sick person. Most of us don't understand how a certain medicine makes us well. We only know that we feel better. God's grace works in a similar and mysterious way. We can never really understand how it leads us to perfection but we know that it does.

So don't worry if you don't understand God and His grace. No amount of reading or studying will ever reveal the answer. Just know that if you are thirsty, you should drink rather than read about water. And if you thirst after His grace, accept it moment by moment rather than reading about it. We should abandon ourselves blindly to accepting and doing God's moment-to-moment tasks to produce fruit that God will help us nourish by sending us more moment-to-moment tasks. Believe with unshaken confidence that God arranges what is best for us at each moment.

Don't fool yourself into thinking you know what's best. Thinking too hard and trying to understand God's intention can lead you astray. When you long for God, He'll provide what you need. Receive His will with simplicity, gentleness, and calm. God will only take full possession of you when you have no confidence in your own reasoning power. Your thoughts merely block and deflect His gifts. Remember

171

without His divine action, you can't make progress toward perfection, and with His grace, nothingness can turn to greatness.

Always focus on the present moment. Wait and expect God's interruptions. Whether you find yourself meditating, praying, reading, doing the laundry, mowing the lawn, or any of a thousand other things, if God sends you something else to do, drop it and regard it as totally unimportant. You should at all times be ready to say, along with St. Paul, "Lord, what will you have me to do?" Don't focus on what you want but on what He wants.

Never fear what tomorrow may bring. The same loving God who cares for you today will take care of you tomorrow and every day. God will either shield you from suffering or give you the strength to bear it.

St. Francis De Sales

Chapter 5

Stay Strong

When the Apostles fled, Mary remained steadfast at the foot of the Cross. She loved Jesus as her Son even after the Romans disfigured Him and covered Him with mud and spittle. The wounds that covered Him made Him more lovable and adorable in the eyes of His tender Mother. The more awful the blasphemies uttered against Him, the deeper her veneration and respect.

A person of strong faith pursues God through all His disguises. They imitate Mary who always, from the stable to the Cross, remained united to Jesus whom so many misunderstood, abandoned, and persecuted. In a similar way, faithful souls endure a constant succession of trials which conceal God's presence and make His will difficult to recognize. However, in spite of every obstacle, these faithful souls follow Him and love Him even to the death on the Cross.

Pursue then, without ceasing, this beloved Spouse and nothing will have power to hide Him from you. He moves above the smallest blades of grass as above the mighty oak.

He walks upon grains of sand as easily as huge mountains. Wherever you turn, there you will find His footprints, and in following them untiringly, you will find Him everywhere.

Oh, what delightful peace you will enjoy when you learn to do these things. Then darkness will provide light and bitterness sweetness. Your faith will change ugliness into beauty and malice to virtue because faith nurtures sweetness, confidence and joy. The faithful feel tenderness and compassion for their enemies who so immeasurably enrich them because the greater the harshness and severity of the situation, the greater the advantage to your soul.

The will of God offers nothing but sweetness, favors and treasures for submissive souls. You cannot place too much confidence in Him. He always acts for, and desires your perfection if you allow Him. Faith never doubts. The more unfaithful, uncertain, and rebellious your senses, the louder faith cries, "All is well, it is the will of God." The eye of faith penetrates the thickest fog, goes straight to the truth, and holds it firmly.

Fr. Jean-Pierre de Caussade suggests we pray this prayer often: "Lord, my mind prefers one thing, my body another, but Lord, I desire only to accomplish Your Holy will. You make everything real and useful by Your will. I devote myself only to Your Holy will because I know that your moment-to-moment graces lead me to perfection."

Remember, contemplation and prayer very often provide opportunities to love and show your esteem to God if you direct this love and esteem entirely to God, who willingly makes use of these means to unite your soul to Himself.

The fire that purifies gold consumes wood; so in the fire of tribulation the just acquire beauty while the wicked turn to ash.

St. John Chrysostom

Chapter 6

Discover the Will of God

At every moment, God places before us things of infinite value, and gives them to us according to the measure of our faith and love. When we learn to see the evidence of God's will in each moment, we find all that our hearts desire. God provides this truth because nothing more reasonable, more perfect, more divine exists than the will of God. No change of time, place, or circumstance can enhance or decrease its infinite value.

Once we know the secret of discovering God's will in every moment and in every thing, we possess the most precious and desirable thing. We know that God fills the present moment with infinite treasure that contains more than we have capacity to carry. God at each moment presents His grace like an immense, inexhaustible ocean that no human heart can fathom. But we can only receive as much as our faith allows. We must strive to increase our faith and thus our capacity to receive more grace. Faith and love are measures. Believe and it will be done to you accordingly. The more the heart loves, the more it desires, and the more it desires, the more it will receive. The divine will is a deep abyss to which the present moment provides the entrance. If we faithfully plunge into this abyss, we find it infinitely more vast than our desires.

Correspondingly, the growth of our faith means the death of our senses. The senses worship earthly things, whereas faith adores the divine. When you sense terror, hunger, or discomfort in any way, then faith grows and strengthens. Faith laughs at calamities like a general of an impregnable fortress laughs at the useless attacks of a weak enemy.

When we recognize and submit to the will of God entirely, then God gives us abundant graces and great comfort. We also experience great happiness because we have learned to abandon ourselves at every moment to His adorable will.

I accept all things as sent to me by the Sacred Heart of Jesus Christ in order to unite myself to Him.

St. Margaret Mary Alacoque

Chapter 7

Embrace the Mystery

God reveals Himself to us in mysterious ways and in ordinary circumstances and as truly and adorably as in the great events of history or Sacred Scripture. God filled His bible with mystery just as He fills the events of the world with incomprehensible mysteries. We only see feeble rays of sunlight obscured by clouds. Darkness takes the place of light, ignorance of knowledge, and we neither see nor understand.

Sacred Scripture contains the mysterious utterances of our mysterious God. He writes the events of this world in the same language that appears as mere drops from an ocean of midnight darkness. The fall of the angels and of Adam and Eve, the impiety and idolatry of men before and after the flood, reveal His will. We see more mysteries with the coming of the Messiah, when only a handful of people accepted Him. In our present time, we see the general ruin and overthrow of faith throughout the world. We see secularism and heresies gaining strength as they powerfully persecute the faithful.

An easy way to become aware of God's presence is to do our ordinary tasks for the love of Him.

Brother Lawrence of the
Resurrection

Chapter 8

Rejoice in God in the Moment

All these mysteries will continue until the end of time to convey His wisdom, power, and goodness. All events of history show His divine attributes and reveal His adorable word. Don't doubt though you don't see. Know that even the enemies of the Church loudly proclaim His perfection. Atheists, non-believers, and the impious exist only for that purpose, but unless you view them through the eye of faith, they have the exact opposite appearance.

To behold divine mysteries we must shut our eyes to the external and stop reasoning. God speaks to us via all public and private events. Every resolution comes as a wave from the sea of His providence, raising storms and tempests in the minds of those who question His mysterious action.

God speaks to everyone through the things happening at every moment of our lives. However, instead of hearing His voice in these events and receiving them with awe, most see only their earthly aspects and object to them. They find fault with everything that happens and nothing pleases them. They judge everything by their senses and by reason, not by faith, the only true standard. They treat God's moment-to-moment manifestations as unworthily as the Jews treated Jesus when He walked the earth.

Infidelity fills the world and many people complain continually about God in language they wouldn't use with the lowest workman. They want to require God to act only within the limits of their feeble reason. They presume to improve His ways.

Not pleased with their situation they say things like, "I don't have enough money or time to do this." Or "No one will let me do this." Or "This illness comes just when I need my health the most." Or "How can a kind and loving God allow this terrible thing to happen?"

God provides only one answer to these objections. We only need Him and nothing else. Therefore, what He doesn't grant must be useless. The things they see as misfortunes, accidents, and disappointments come from God. They blaspheme God when they reject and flee from them. People who don't attach themselves solely to the will of God find neither satisfaction nor sanctification in any other thing they do, no matter how excellent.

If what God chooses for you does not content you, where else do you expect to find it? If the meal prepared for you doesn't please you, what other food can? Only accomplishing the tasks of the present moment can nourish, fortify, purify, enrich, and sanctify you. Here you find all good and have no reason to seek it elsewhere. To resist this truth causes all our troubles. If books, the example of the saints, and spiritual conversations fill your mind without satisfying it, you have strayed from the path of pure abandonment to God's will. You seek only to please yourself. To act this way blocks God's grace and you must stop immediately.

God wants you to focus and handle what He sends each moment because all good things come from God. Remember that God always speaks mysteriously and we often fail to comprehend. His mysteriousness makes us live by faith, for all else ends in contradiction. The more you feel the death of sense and reason, the stronger your faith should grow. The more obscure the mystery, the more light it contains. Thus, simple souls discover the most meaning in things that appear to have the least meaning because a life of faith requires a continual struggle against the senses.

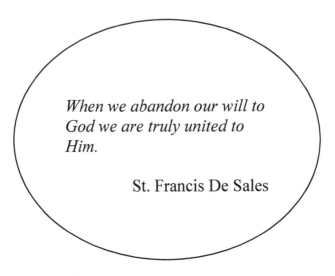

When we abandon our will to God we are truly united to Him.

St. Francis De Sales

Chapter 9

The Gospel in Our Heart

God continues to write in the hearts of men the work He began in the Holy Scriptures, but we will only read the text and understand its meaning on the day of judgment. From the beginning of the world, God created us and has participated as man from the first instant of His incarnation. During the whole course of our lives, He acts within our souls. For Him, the time that will elapse until the end of the world passes like a single day and all abounds with His actions.

In the Bible, the Holy Spirit reveals some of the more important moments in that ocean of time. In them we see some of the mysterious ways God the Father brought Jesus to the world. We see His origin, race, and genealogy. The whole of the Old Testament outlines the profound mystery of this Divine work and contains all the necessary facts to relate the advent of Jesus Christ. The Holy Spirit has kept all the rest hidden among the treasures of His wisdom.

From this ocean of divine activity, He only allows a tiny stream to escape, and this stream then vanishes in the Apostles and ends in the Apocalypse. Only with faith can we understand the history of Jesus' activity with the faithful.

The Holy Spirit continues to carry on the work of our Savior. While helping the Church to preach the Gospel of Jesus Christ, He writes His own Gospel in the hearts of the faithful. Every action, every moment of their lives reflects the Gospel of the Holy Spirit. The souls of the saints represent the paper, the sufferings and actions, the ink. The Holy Spirit with the pen of His power writes a living Gospel, but a Gospel that we can't read until it has left the press of this life and God publishes it on the day of eternity.

The press still runs, and every day He adds more text and prints more pages. However, we all remain in the dark night of faith with the paper blacker than the ink and the words jumbled. If we could see clearly, we'd understand how God animates and guides everyone in different ways to the same goal. We'd see that all has meaning and connection to His work. But we can't read a book written in a mysterious language and with pages all blotted with ink.

God sends His love to us under veils like the Eucharistic species. What great truths hide from Christians who imagine themselves enlightened? How many of them understand that every cross, every action, everything that attracts or repels them comes from God as a gift to lead them to perfection. God makes use of both pleasant and bad situations. Our love for Him gains for us greater graces when we joyfully accept repugnant situations. Though certainly not a sacrament with sanctifying grace, we can experience it moment by moment throughout the day. Consequently, the more holy the life we lead, the more mysterious it becomes by its apparent simplicity and littleness.

Fr. Jean-Pierre de Caussade encourages us to pray, "Guide me, Lord, as I desire to become your disciple and like

184

a little child believe what I cannot understand and cannot see. I take comfort knowing You speak to me moment by moment. You say this and show that. You arrange all in Your own way. You make yourself heard and I accept it all. I do not see the reason, but believe in your infallible truth and know that all You say and do remains forever true. I know that all that appears complicated, perplexing, foolish, inconsistent, and imaginary will ultimately entrance and delight me by its order, knowledge, wisdom and incomprehensible wonder."

At every moment God places before us things of infinite value and then gives them to us according to our faith.

Fr. Jean-Pierre de Caussade

Chapter 10

It's Just for You

God sends to us moment by moment the most useful things because He intends them especially for us. He knows that we learn the most from lessons tailored to our needs. We gain little wisdom by reading books, which mostly confuse and fill us with pride. We learn best by experience and actions, where He speaks life-giving words. Thus, reading only brings wisdom when God sends us the task of reading. If we read with a sense of pride or because we want to but we know we should serve God in another way, we become like foolish guides who know all the roads in their area but who lose their way going home.

We must listen to God moment to moment to understand His practical theology of virtue. Don't do tasks intended for others, but listen carefully for your own. God will send you enough to exercise your faith because He wishes to purify and increase your faith in His moment-to-moment mysterious way.

We don't have far to go to quench our thirst. God's grace flows quite close in each present moment. With His river of grace so near, we don't have to go thirsty. Chasing after what we deem important will only increases our thirst. To think, to write, and to speak like the prophets, the Apostles, and the Saints, we must give ourselves up, as they did, to the inspirations of God.

When we do this, we discover that God provides an inexhaustible supply of new thoughts, fresh sufferings, joys, and needed actions for those who have no need to copy the lives of others, but only to live in perpetual abandonment to God moment to moment.

What an incomplete understanding of the Faith we have if we only study the Bible or read about saints or church history. Since the time of Adam and Eve, God has worked at every instant, filling, sanctifying, and super-naturalizing every moment. This ancient method of abandonment to divine providence always provides a sure path. The saints of the first ages understood the secret of doing God's will in the moment. This gift, still present today, never ceases to pour forth its grace on those who abandon themselves to it without reserve.

The perfection of our souls and the degree of excellence we attain depends on our faithfulness to the order established by God. God gives graces to those who submit to His will by performing the duties of the moment. God makes saints as He pleases, but according to His plan and in submission to His will. Such submission provides true and perfect abandonment. The more completely we submit, the higher our sanctity.

Never think that great and powerful people who have influence over thousands or millions of people achieve greater sanctity than ordinary people. From the moment we receive our duties from God and begin to perform them, we move closer to perfection no matter the duty and no matter our state of life. We find perfection by submitting unreservedly to the designs of God, and in fulfilling our duties as perfectly as possible.

Comparing different states and duties provides no benefit because neither the amount of work nor the type of duty matters when striving for perfection. God measures holiness in the love we have for Him and our desire to please Him. We see this in Jesus, Mary and Joseph. They each had more love for God than any other quality. They sought holiness not in things, but only in how and why they used them. Therefore, we know that one way doesn't provide a better path to perfection than another. All ways can lead to perfection if they conform to God's will in His moment-to-moment manner of reaching out to us.

Give your heart to God and your hands to work.

St. Mary Joseph Rossello

Chapter 11

You Can Do It!

Abandonment to divine providence enabled Job to bless the name of God in his utter desolation. Instead of looking upon his condition as ruin, he called it the name of God. By blessing it, he proclaimed it the Holy divine will of God, no matter that it came in the form of terrible catastrophes. Our continual recognition of the will of God, as manifested and revealed in all things, shows that He reigns in us, that He does His will on earth as in Heaven, and that He nourishes our souls in this way.

To understand God's will we must remain quietly amenable to it. None of our efforts, speculations, intelligence, or cleverness helps. Only passive abandonment and yielding to it like metal in a mold, or a canvas to the brush of the artist, or the stone in the hands of a sculptor leads to perfection.

Wise and just people find contentment in what God intends for them. Such people know to confine themselves within the boundary of their path and not to go beyond its limits. They don't inquire into God's ways but they content themselves with His will and make no effort to discover His meaning, and only focus on what the moment reveals. They listen to the depths of their heart and don't concern themselves with what God reveals to others, but remain satisfied with what they receive moment by moment.

In this way they gain a perfectly simple and absolutely solid spirituality. They don't do things based on their own ideas, which would only serve to excite pride. Pious people make a great use of their minds, but people abandoned to divine providence have little use for mental exertion and find it antagonistic to true piety. We must make use only of that which God sends us to do or to suffer, and not forsake this divine reality to occupy our minds with historical wonders of divine work. By staying focused on His divine will we make our way along the path to perfection.

Fr. Jean-Pierre de Caussade believed we can easily learn about the graces hidden in the daily duties of our state of life. That we can find happiness and sanctity in our daily duties and that the safest and surest path to perfection lies in accepting the crosses sent by Providence at every moment. That true wisdom lies in submitting to the will of God, which transforms all troubles and sufferings into divine gold.

We should take great comfort in knowing that to acquire God's friendship and to reach Heaven, we must, in a Holy manner, merely do what we normally do, suffer what we routinely suffer, and know that what we think of as unimportant pleases God far more than extraordinary deeds and wonderful works.

Each station of life has its own duties; when we do them well we find happiness.

St. Nicholas of Flute

About the Authors

The Venerable Louis of Granada, O.P.

Louis of Granada remains peerless among Dominican ascetical writers, and throughout the seventeenth century he inspired and taught Christians throughout the civilized world. Because he focused primarily on ordinary people a contemporary writer said, "Water girls carry his books under their arms and the market women read them as they wait to sell their merchandise."

Louis of Granada preached traditional Christian values focused on the perfection of charity. Many saints from the sixteenth and seventeenth centuries devoutly read his books. These included St. Teresa of Avila, St. John of the Cross, St. Charles Borromeo, St. Peter Alcántara, St. Rose of Lima, St. Francis de Sales and St. Louise de Marillac.

St. Francis de Sales recommended Granada to a bishop-elect by saying, "I urge you to have on hand the complete works of Louis of Granada and to use them as a second breviary. Derive profit from them by slowly pondering them chapter by chapter meditating with much attention and prayers to God. They must be read with reverence and devotion as books that contain the most useful inspirations."

Father Jean-Pierre de Caussade, S.J.

Jean-Pierre de Caussade was born in France in 1675. He was ordained in 1708 and for the next six years taught grammar, physics, and logic in the French Jesuit college in Toulouse after which he became a missionary and preacher.

His spirituality, heavily influenced by St. Francis de Sales and St John of the Cross, combines the teaching of self-abandonment and simplicity of St. Francis with the Carmelite view of grace as purifying and enlightening the soul.

The Rev. Jean Pierre de Caussade, a deeply spiritual man, practiced what he preached, abandonment to God. De Caussade taught to accept and welcome whatever happens to you at every moment as flowing directly from God. Furthermore, he taught that though you might not always get the things you want, you'll have peace. He will teach you that you can do no better than to follow step-by-step the course appointed to you by divine providence.

A Final Note from Brother Bob

I hope you've found this book helpful and that it will make a difference in your life. Perhaps it made you think of someone in your family, a friend, a neighbor, or a chance acquaintance, someone who needs to make the teachings of this book part of their life. And in truth, that's probably all of us. If that is indeed the case, give them this book and become Brother Bob yourself.

If you feel uncomfortable with gifting this volume, I encourage you to go to my blog for suggestions on how to pass it along anonymously. I'd also like for you to share your stories about this book, its teachings, and how you've passed on the wisdom of these words on my blog. That URL is brotherbobsblog.wordpress.com.

I hope to see you there.

Brother Bob

To order additional copies of this book
The Sinner's Guide and
Abandonment to Divine Providence

Name_____

Address _____

_____

_____

$9.95 x _____ copies = _____

Sales Tax _____
(Texas residents add 8.25% sales tax)

Please add $3.50 postage and handling _____

Total amount due: _____

We offer a quantity discount. For every 4 books you order, we'll send a 5th book free.

Please send check or money order for books to:

WordWright.biz
46561 State Highway 118
WordWright Business Park
Alpine, Texas 79830

For a complete catalog of books,
visit our site at
http://www.WordWright.biz

Lightning Source UK Ltd.
Milton Keynes UK
UKHW01f0620260618
324800UK00001B/284/P